TRUST &
BETRAYAL

TRUST & BETRAYAL

Dawnings of Consciousness

Published under the auspices of
ISAPZURICH
(International School of
Analytical Psychology Zürich)
AGAP Post-Graduate Jungian Training

Edited by
Stacy Wirth, Isabelle Meier, & John Hill

Spring Journal Books
New Orleans, Louisiana

Published by
Spring Journal, Inc.
627 Ursulines Street #7
New Orleans, Louisiana 70116
Tel.: (504) 524-5117
Website: www.springjournalandbooks.com

Cover design:
Stacy Wirth

Cover layout & typesetting:
Northern Graphic Design & Publishing
info@ncarto.com

Cover photograph:
Dawn at Lake Lucerne
Courtesy of Fritz Bieri, www.beatenbergbilder

Printed in USA
Text printed on acid-free paper

Library of Congress Cataloging-in-Publication Data Pending

DEDICATION

*This book is dedicated to all who
undertake the epic voyage of soul, in particular to
the students, analysts, and visitors of ISAPZURICH,
who gathered from all over the world in Gersau
to discuss the quandaries of trust and betrayal.*

Contents

Acknowledgments

Once again our deepest gratitude extends to Nancy Cater for her publication of the Jungian Odyssey Series as well as her support of the Jungian Odyssey from year to year. We are most pleased that Nancy has joined the Jungian Odyssey Committee as our Honorary Advisor. We are indebted to Kate Babbitt, our copy-editor, for her diligent accompaniment of our publication process.

The publication of this series depends also on the success of the Jungian Odyssey as an event, which goes forward thanks to the efforts of more individuals than we can name here. We mention especially Katy Remark for her ongoing participation as a member of the Jungian Odyssey Committee; Karin Buchser, for her support as ISAP's Director of Operations; Helga Kopecky, ISAP's librarian, who faithfully provides a rich supply of literature for our bookshop; Andrew Fellows, a recent ISAP graduate, who joined us for the first time this year to take charge of onsite technical matters and to lend his skills as DJ at our gala closing party. Our great thanks as well to those ISAP candidates who took time out from training to assist our efforts: Mary Tomlinson (Canada) for her fair-minded attention to course allocations; Isolde Kunerth (Germany) for her technical support; and Eleonora Babejova (Slovakia) and Susanne Bucher (Switzerland) for managing book sales.

Stacy Wirth, Isabelle Meier, John Hill
2011

About the Jungian Odyssey

The International School of Analytical Psychology Zürich (ISAPZURICH) has been conducting postgraduate training since 2004, the year it was established by the Association of Graduate Analytical Psychologists (AGAP), which was founded in 1954. AGAP itself is a founding member and the largest member society of the International Association for Analytical Psychology (IAAP).

Since 2006 the Jungian Odyssey has taken place each spring semester as an off-campus retreat, an arrangement that opens ISAP's program to all who are interested in C. G. Jung and analytical psychology. In keeping with the Homeric journey, the Odyssey travels from year to year, finding "harbor" in different regions of Switzerland and drawing thematic inspiration from the landscapes that so influenced Jung's sense of psyche. ISAP was honored to begin collaborating with Spring Journal Books in 2008, when Nancy Cater proposed the publication of an annual series based upon each year's Odyssey lectures. After the Jungian Odyssey 2008, which took place in Beatenberg, the series was launched with the publication of *Intimacy: Venturing the Uncertainties of the Heart* (2009), followed by *Destruction and Creation: Facing the Ambiguities of Power* (2010).

Introduction:
Dawnings of Consciousness

Stacy Wirth, Isabelle Meier, John Hill

"The earth has a spirit of her own." C. G. Jung[1]

The fifth Jungian Odyssey, and this volume of essays, were inspired by Rütli Meadow, which lies in the heart of Switzerland on the north shore of Uri, one of Switzerland's mythical three founding cantons. A small and secluded grassy plateau in the forest, Rütli is accessible only on foot or by a boat trip on the Lake of the Four Forest Cantons.[2] Rarely peopled, the meadow is kept today primarily for cattle grazing. It features a semicircle of massive old stone benches nestled beneath a stand of enormous pine trees and yews. At the lakeside border of the meadow, the waters of three tiny springs trickle down from a simple limestone embankment. To those who listen attentively, the three springs whisper the story of a mystical happening linked to the dawning of Swiss democracy and the Old Confederation.[3]

At first glance this idyllic meadow resembles some kind of Eden, an island of blissful containment, a *temenos* of primal trust. It evokes a quality of being that we yearn for and live with our lovers, our friends, our family, and our analysts and that we sometimes find in relationships with larger social groups, leaders, and institutions. Quintessentially first realized in the bond of mother and child, primal trust forms a bedrock from which flows self-trust, individual autonomy, and trust in the world. Abraham Maslow, stressing the psychological necessity, goes so far as to assert that "trust in the self and trust in the world" lie behind our capacity to open to "mystery . . . the unfamiliar . . . the ambiguous and contradictory," for it is trust that "permits the temporary giving up of straining and striving, of volition and control, of conscious effort."[4]

Yet to follow the Swiss founding myth is to realize that Rütli Meadow symbolizes so much more. Its meaning would be incomplete without the mythic narrative of the indigenous valley people. Defying oppression by the foreign bailiffs, who murdered their neighbors, abused their women, seized their houses, and stole their cattle, they took a secret oath to renew local trust and to plan rebellion. "We vow eternally as comrades to aid one another and defend against all evil-doers," declared the three oath-takers who represented the valley dwellers. "And never again will we bow to foreign judges, but yield only to the most prudent among our own!"[5] When the oath was sworn at Rütli Meadow on a dark night in 1291, so the myth goes, three tiny springs spouted forth at the oath-takers' feet. It wasn't long before a related legend had sprung up around the freedom fighter Wilhelm Tell, who defied, tricked, and killed the cruelest bailiff of them all and so ignited the great uprising. The bailiffs' castles were set ablaze and the tyrants were driven out of the valleys. And Rütli Meadow became consecrated ground, echoing the story of the Confederation's birth.[6]

At the end of July 1940, as Switzerland's neighbors capitulated to Nazi Germany, the Swiss commander-in-chief, Henri Guisan, struck the chords of a collective soul deeply when he summoned his commanding officers to Rütli Meadow. Bidding his men to "hear the mysterious call from the past which comes from [this] place," Guisan kindled the nation's spiritual resolve to stand together against the enemy threat:[7]

> We can only respect those who are determined to resist and know how to do it. . . . If it is true that all signs of weakness on our part are being used against us, it is equally true that all signs of strength proclaim our unflinching determination to stand firm.[8]

Did Switzerland stand firm against the enemy? Later research, particularly by the Bergier commission, tells another story.[9] The "mysterious call from the past" was soon betrayed. The Swiss made secret agreements with the Nazis, money was laundered, trade continued as usual, and transportation of vital goods was guaranteed, all to support the Axis alliance. Switzerland had lost her innocence.

In Rütli Meadow's mythic and "mysterious call" we discern certain psychological facts that have been conveyed through the ages in so many archetypal narratives. Trust contains the seed of betrayal—and without betrayal, trust amounts to little more than capture in a state of naive, child-like bliss. If dwelling in trust lends us the feeling of being whole, without the rupture of trust we remain incomplete. Few among us would wish to betray or to be betrayed; we would sooner sidestep the wounding, the "aweful and luminous" experience, as Jean Houston puts it.[10] And yet, as Houston observes,

> [Betrayal] marks the expulsion from Eden into the empirical but evolutionary world of consciousness, growth, autonomy, responsibility. It is only through losing by betrayal our sense of intimate linkage with the other—be it mother or father or family or friend—and are thrust out into unprotected existence, that we really begin to grow. . . . For all its negativity, betrayal is an advance over primal trust, for it leads to evolution and growth and the many extensions of love; it extends the universe in its challenges and vicissitudes; it grows the world and ourselves.[11]

Looking through the lens of Jung's analytical psychology, the contributors to this volume illuminate the motifs of trust and betrayal as a ubiquitous, archetypal pair that bears on private and collective life as well as on clinical practice. Self-trust and trust in others are essential to our sense of a unified and ongoing existence. But trust can be blind, amounting to psychological stagnation and to unconscious self-betrayal and the betrayal of others. Thus, to betray or to suffer betrayal can be necessary if also distressing pathways to individuation. In Jung's succinct words, "There is no birth of consciousness without pain."[12]

NOTES

[1] C. G. Jung, *Visions: Notes of the Seminar Given in 1930–1934,* ed. Claire Douglas (London: Routledge, 1998), 1:133.

[2] In English this lake is more popularly known by the name Lake of Lucerne.

[3] We are grateful to ISAP analyst Brigitte Egger for leading the Odyssey excursion to Rütli Meadow and its surrounds. It was a special privilege to share this and other events with the African healers Jane Bedford, Charmaine Joseph, and Alexandra Otto, whose attendance of the Odyssey was made possible by ISAP analyst Peter Ammann. We regret that due to space limitations, their spontaneous contributions cannot be included in this volume.

[4] Abraham H. Maslow, *The Farther Reaches of Human Nature* (New York: Penguin Books, 1971), pp. 64–65.

⁵ Our paraphrase, based on the Federal Charter of 1291, available at "The Federal Authorities of the Swiss Convention," http://www.admin.ch/org/polit/00056/index.html?lang=en. The legend of the Rütli Oath is first mentioned in *The White Book of Sarnen* (1470).

⁶ For a telling of the myth, see "Tell, William," in *Classic Encyclopedia*, http://www.1911encyclopedia.org/William_Tell. The *Classic Encyclopedia* website is based on Hugh Chisholm, ed., *Encyclopaedia Britannica*, 11th ed. (Cambridge: Cambridge University Press, 1911); the Tell entry is in volume 26, p. 574.

⁷ Henri Guisan, quoted in E. Bonjour, H. S. Offler, and G. R. Potter, *A Short History of Switzerland* (Oxford: Clarendon Press, 1952), p. 371.

⁸ *Ibid.*

⁹ Commission indépendante d'experts Suisse—Seconde guerre mondiale, *Switzerland, National Socialism and the Second World War: Final Report of the Independent Commission of Experts*, trans. Rosmund Bandi, Hillary Crowe, Ian Tickle, and Susan Worthington (Zurich: Pendo Verlag, 2002).

¹⁰ Jean Houston, "Pathos and Soul Making," in *Carl Jung and Soul Psychology*, ed. Karin Gibson, Donald Lathrop, and E. Mark Stern (Binghamton, N.Y.: Harrington Park Press, 1991), p. 75.

¹¹ *Ibid.*, pp. 78, 80.

¹² C. G. Jung, "Marriage as a Psychological Relationship" (1931), in *The Development of Personality*, vol. 17 of *The Collected Works of C. G. Jung*, ed. Herbert Read, Michael Fordham, Gerhard Adler, and William McGuire, trans. R. F. C. Hull (Princeton, N.J.: Princeton University Press, 1977), §331.

1

Betrayal:
A Way to Wisdom?

Murray Stein

INTRODUCTION

Betrayal, one of the themes of this Jungian Odyssey, hovering above the subtitle "Dawnings of Consciousness," is a timely topic. The news is filled these days with cries of betrayal of trust and the troubled dawnings of consciousness that trust has been misplaced and misused. Example: the famous credit ratings agencies, Moody's, Standard & Poor's, and Fitch, are currently under investigation on charges that they colluded with banks to mislead investors about the creditworthiness of government bonds in Greece, Portugal, and Spain (among other nations). If investors can't trust their money with these venerable institutions, where can they turn? Consciousness is dawning today that many previously trusted institutions, like banks (including the big Swiss ones!) and governments, are not what they seem. The personae created by and for them do not reveal true intentions but instead conceal the shadow forces of greed that reign in their hidden precincts and busily invent new strategies of betrayal.

We should not be so surprised by the behavior of today's bankers, however. In the New Testament, the most infamous example of betrayal is Judas, the disciple who handled the finances for the devoted group of disciples around Jesus. In his act of betrayal, when he "delivered up" (in Latin this is expressed by the word *tradere,* from which descends the English word "betray") the Lord to the Romans, he displayed for posterity the archetypal image of the flawed moneyman. Wisdom counsels caution when sitting with people who deal with money.

It can be one short step from trust to cynicism when one considers the betrayal behavior of human beings who have had power through the ages. Power and desire corrupt integrity. The current controversy burning through the Catholic Church about predatory priests who have betrayed their sacrosanct positions for the sake of sexual pleasure at the expense of children has led more than a few people to question the sincerity of clerics at all levels and in all places. Many are leaving the church as a result, sneering at allusions to any possibility of goodness in human motives. Those who were abused are filled with rage and have risen up to call for transparency. Will the traumas inflicted upon them as children and youths drive them into cynicism?

We must recognize that the benefits of the idealizing transference are hard for its recipients to resist, whether they be priests, analysts, golf champions, or just simple men or women who are admired and loved too well. Transference objects, be they gods or humans, are dangerous to keep around because of the trust we place in them. The cynic is one who knows this all too well, having been deeply wounded and unwilling to let go of the pain inflicted. Instead, he or she hangs on to pain and reinterprets the world through the eyes of mistrust, even paranoia. Betrayal has shattered the cynic's capacity to imagine a decent relationship. No more do hands reach out for attachment; there is no inner space for faith, no capacity left for love. The world has turned into a valley of pain where shadows beckon and promise fulfillment but deliver only misery and death.

Is there another possible outcome? Can betrayal lead to wisdom instead of to cynicism? This is a possibility I wish to consider, and to that end I propose the following:

> Betrayal shatters images that consciousness has built up into seemingly reliable structures in which one can place faith and trust. Out of this shattering of trusted images, which leads to profound darkness and despair, a light of new consciousness may emerge that we would call wisdom.

Consider the ancient question posed by Job: "But where shall wisdom be found?"[1] I am venturing here to speak of a possible way to wisdom in the alchemy of psychological development that begins with trust broken, which then passes into the state of *nigredo* and moves on through this stage of darkness to the *albedo* of wisdom—from naïveté to maturity, from *Songs of Innocence* to *Songs of Experience,* from consciousness based on *belief* to consciousness grounded in *knowledge*. I would never say that this is inevitable, but I would like to explore the psychological conditions that make it possible.

The emergence of new consciousness into a state of wisdom through the doorway of betrayal depends, of course, on the psychological survival of the betrayed. Some victims of betrayal, like Desdemona in Shakespeare's *Othello* or Julius Caesar, whom Brutus famously betrays, do not live to see the dawning of a new day.

"In God We Trust"

If we take betrayal to the ultimate—to its classical apex—we have to consider the greatest betrayal of all, the betrayal of a blameless man by God Himself. I must confess that it will forever remain a wonder to me that the biblical redactors allowed what appears to be such a subversive work into the canon. Doesn't this book blatantly question the faith and trust the community is supposed to place in the Lord with whom they have a Covenant, a sacred contract of mutuality?

Here is the problem. In the fifth book of the Pentateuch, Deuteronomy, the Lord swears for all to hear:

> And because you hearken to these ordinances, and keep and do them, the Lord your God will keep with you the covenant and the steadfast love which he swore to your fathers to keep; he will love you, bless you, and multiply you; he will also bless the fruit of your body and the fruit of your ground, your grain and your wine and your oil, the increase of your cattle and the young of your flock, in the land which he swore to your fathers to give you. You shall be blessed above all peoples.[2]

This is the promise God made to Israel.

In the book of Job, however, the Lord unaccountably takes a contrary position. First he praises his servant Job as faultless, hence his enviable prosperity as represented by his ten children; his thousands of sheep, camels, oxen, and she-asses; and his many servants. He is the richest man of the east, and the Lord is pleased to have kept his promise as stated in the Covenant above. But when wily Satan challenges Job's sincerity, God yields to Satan's seduction: "Behold, he is in your power; only spare his life" (Job 2:9). With that, he delivers his faithful servant Job into the hands of the architect of ruin and destruction for a test. Job has done nothing to call for this unfair trial. Is this not a betrayal of the Covenant?

So what is the Bible trying to say with the inclusion of the book of Job? Let's remember that it belongs to what in Biblical Studies is called wisdom literature. Thus, we need to consider the role of betrayal in the attainment of wisdom.

Jung's *Answer to Job*

In his astonishing late work *Answer to Job*, Jung draws some startling conclusions from the presence of the book of Job in the biblical canon.[3] Here I will give only the briefest review of his argument, then I will discuss how this work played a part in a betrayal story that unfolded in Jung's relationship with the English Dominican priest Victor White and how that episode relates to the attainment of wisdom.

Jung's interpretation of the book of Job has often been cause for wonder and sometimes for extremely sharp criticism. It is said that when he was asked what he thought of it, Karl Barth, the great Swiss theologian and Jung's contemporary, commented wryly that the book says more about the mind of the psychologist than about the mind of God. He was of course passing judgment from the Olympian heights of theology. As a Protestant Christian theologian of note, he could speak with some certainty of what lies in the mind of God, whereas Jung was limited to mere human knowledge and psychology. One must remember that Jung is writing as a working psychotherapist, so his antennae are tuned differently from those of a theologian or biblical scholar. Jung's essay is not a work of biblical theology, although it does touch deeply upon the psychological sources for theological perception and thinking, namely the mythic developments within the books of the Bible. In his bold text, Jung puts himself in the position of a psychotherapist listening to a patient's story.

The protagonist, Job, presents himself as an utterly pious man, innocent of any conscious or unconscious faults or sins. God agrees with this assessment. As He looks down upon his servant from his heavenly throne, He praises him as a perfect example of virtue and obedience to the laws of the Covenant, a wholly pious and blameless man. Satan, the Lord's sly interlocutor, challenges this perception and offers to put it to the test. He claims that if God's servant Job is stripped of his possessions, his family, his health, and all that has gone into his rich and successful life, he will become cynical, betray his faith, and turn his back on the Lord. So God takes the bait and lets Satan do his worst, stipulating only that he spare Job's life.

And thus the horrible story unfolds. Job loses his children, all of his wealth, and his health. At this point his wife tells him to curse God and die. He refuses and declares in the famous lines: "For I know that my Redeemer lives, and at last he will stand upon the earth; and after my skin has been thus destroyed, then from my flesh I shall see God, whom I shall see on my side, and my eyes shall behold, and not another."[4] He turns a deaf ear to the friends who argue that he is being punished for some breach in his supposedly righteous conduct, stubbornly defending his innocence and faultlessness.

Finally, the Lord answers Job in a great display of majesty and power, showing him his pitiful smallness as a man compared to His supreme authority as God Almighty, Creator of Heaven and Earth. Job is silenced. He does not raise the slightest objection to what the Lord has done to him, and in no way does he accuse God of betraying him. Instead, he receives this awesome show of power in silence and humility. After this, God restores his wealth, gives him a new set of children, and puts things back in order for him.

As Jung the psychotherapist listened to this story, he became enraged. He experienced what Michael Fordham called a syntonic countertransference.[5] He speaks up for Job's repressed feelings of anger and outrage at being so unfairly played with by God. As a deeply tuned and empathic psychotherapist, Jung registered the unconscious feelings of Job, and in his impassioned text he voiced them boldly and without reservation. Going a step further in his role as psychoanalyst, he diagnosed this deity as being dissociated from his omniscience, as split off from his anima and from Eros, and as abysmally unconscious and lacking in integration as a personality. Basically, he depicted the Lord of the book of Job as exhibiting the features of a narcissistic or borderline personality, lacking in reflection and the capacity to contain his impulses and totally incapable of empathizing with the troubles inflicted by his own left hand (Satan) on his victim. In other words, Jung depicted the Lord as the Great Betrayer and Job, an innocent victim, as the betrayed. And this made him very angry. He was in the grips of a profound countertransference reaction, and he let fly with all his emotion. (Victor White took Jung to task for this display of raw emotion. He called it a piece of "childish ignorance"[6] and accused Jung of a "public parade of splenetic shadow."[7])

There is no doubt that what happened to Job is not fair, so how can justice be served? Jung asked. God must be held to account. This is the surprising turn of events, unanticipated by the Lord who thought that only Job was being tested, whereas in reality He too is under scrutiny. Jung demanded justice, compensation, a balancing of accounts. Yes, Job has a replacement family and a new fortune, but this can hardly make up for what he lost. Job may have survived, but now justice must still be done and a new consciousness must be born. To this end, God the betrayer must be made to suffer precisely what He has inflicted on Job. God must become conscious, and the only way to consciousness is through an equivalent experience. Therefore, God must suffer what Job has suffered, namely betrayal of the deepest and most devastating sort. And God must do this to Himself, since no one could of course do this to Him.

Consequently, God incarnates himself as a man, as Jesus of Nazareth. Jung interprets the story of the New Testament as a direct reaction to the betrayal God inflicted on Job. Jesus, the incarnation of God, will experience what Job was made to experience, and through this suffering God will satisfy the requirement of justice and become conscious. The experiences of betrayal that Jesus is put through—not only that of Judas, but the betrayal by God as expressed in the words Jesus uttered on Golgotha: "My God, my God, why hast Thou forsaken me?"—are God's sufferings in parallel to those of Job, and these comprise the *Answer to Job*. In this reprise of the story, Jesus is the savior of God, not mankind.

Like Job, Jesus survives the betrayal. He resurrects and ascends to heaven. So in neither case does the story descend into cynicism and a complete breakdown of faith and trust, to a vision of reality that is devoid of trustworthiness and in which there is no redemption. According to Jung, God should have attained wisdom through this experience of betrayal.

A psychologist, however, must ask: Are these outcomes satisfactory? Do they convey psychological truth? Or are they illusory, defensive, and a mere flimsy patchwork placed over the deep wound of betrayal? Jung the psychotherapist did not buy into the view that all ends well in these parallel narratives. The betrayal is too deep. (In his writings, Jung rarely spoke of the resurrection and the ascension. Easter was not his favorite holiday. Good Friday was more convincing.) For Jung, who was listening to the story of the Bible unfold from his psychotherapeutic chair, the story of Job ends with the revelation of God's awesome power that silences the human, and the story of Jesus concludes on the note of betrayal cried out from the cross. He will not be drawn into an illusory solution, a *folie à deux* with the patient that says everything is okay when in fact it is not. As a psychotherapist, he insists on staying with the *nigredo* state until it transforms from within. No magical solutions are allowed, no easy escapes, no defensive flights into fantasy. The tragedy of betrayal must be fully digested before it can transform into wisdom.

So Jung presses on. One has to come to a state of consciousness that can positively accept and contain evil alongside the good. To simply flee into the good is to set up what Donald Kalsched, following Fordham, has called a defense of the self; that is, a defensive structure that is meant to protect the soul from the insult of deep betrayal but does this job at a price too high.[8] The naïve believer in a happy outcome for this story gets stuck in the defense of religious belief in the good. Such a person cannot cope with the evil within and without. This is a trap with enormous consequences for the individual and for society, as we see in our fundamentalistic age. It isolates the soul from life and from further experience. The consequence is spiritual deadness, stagnation. Jung wanted something better for his patients. He wanted to preserve the possibility of life, and to that end he advocated going further into the suffering.

Betrayal shatters the precious and often sacrosanct images a person has lived by, hoped in, found guidance from, and trusted. The idealized transference object is broken and another reality is presented, a reality that shows the shadow beside the persona, the depths of pathology in the human condition alongside its nobility and glory, the brutally destructive element in God beside the creative, the hateful beside the loving. It is a hard vision to bear, but it is the only way to go on from betrayal toward wisdom and further life.

This is what Jung discovered in his midlife confrontation with the unconscious as recorded in the recently published *Red Book.* As he said in conversation (probably more than once), every bowl of soup has a hair in it. This is the voice of wisdom. It doesn't mean you shouldn't eat soup ever again. Just beware before you put the spoon into your mouth.

Jung espoused the theological image resulting from this psychotherapeutic analysis and treatment as a vision of God as a union of opposites.[9] God is to be seen as a *complexio oppositorum,* a unified complexity that includes good and evil. And it was precisely on this point that his relationship with Victor White foundered.

C. G. JUNG AND FR. VICTOR WHITE, O.P.

If you watch the performance of *The Jung-White Letters*[10] featuring Paul Brutsche in the role of C. G. Jung and John Hill as Victor White, O.P., you will witness the trajectory of a relationship begun in the summer of 1945, just after the end of World War II, with high hopes and enthusiasm about collaboration between the psychologist and the Roman Catholic theologian. The arc of their collaboration and friendship rises with rapid acceleration to a zenith (around 1948), then begins to founder when they enter into a more earnest exchange of views on the nature of God and on the Roman Catholic doctrine of evil as *privatio boni* (1949–1955). The friendship loses its basis and falls into severe disarray and finally into a rupture around what Victor White perceived as a betrayal and Jung saw as an unwarranted attack from White on his integrity. White's sense of betrayal stemmed from Jung's publication of *Answer to Job.* White wrote bitterly to

Jung after the book was published and translated into English: "I wonder what induced you to publish it; when you gave me the MS. to read you were so emphatic that you would not!"[11] Earlier he had found the work fascinating, but when he had to answer pointed questions about its contents from his priest-colleagues and his Catholic followers and analysands, he became extremely uncomfortable and felt that Jung had cut the ground out from under him with the publication of this heterodox work.

Certainly from a Roman Catholic theological perspective rooted in the teachings of St. Thomas Aquinas, which White knew backward and forward and had taught to seminarians for many years, Jung's views were completely indefensible and out of bounds. How could he, a priest, work with Catholic students and analysands when the founder of the psychology he was using and had been advocating was putting forward a view of God and the Bible and what must be done by modern men and women that so utterly contradicted what the Church would ever condone? White found himself strangely in the position of Job when betrayed by God—the very basis of his livelihood and professional existence was pulled out from under his feet. Unlike Job, however, he vented his rage with the transference object, C. G. Jung, and separated himself from him, going his own way: "It seems that I am destined to be a wanderer & as homeless physically as I am spiritually."[12] Ironically, in publishing *Answer to Job,* Jung repeated almost exactly the very thing his book dealt with so passionately—betrayal.

Perhaps it was inadvertent. From White's side, it must have seemed like the betrayal of a faithful and pious man (i.e., himself) at the hands of a mistakenly idealized transference object (i.e., Jung). Jung responded to White's letter of accusation by saying that he had never promised such a thing: "Should I set the light of such an insight 'under a bushel'"? he cried out.[13] He felt heavily burdened with an urgent message for humanity, which he felt was especially needed in a time when humanity, now armed with atomic bombs, was on the verge of catastrophic splitting and self-destruction. He was advocating for consciousness, for individual responsibility, for maturity. Only under such advances in humanity would the world survive, he felt. And White was trying to protect an illusion that robbed people of their initiative, that diminished their consciousness of individual responsibility, and had been helpless to prevent the European nations from entering into two horrific wars in the twentieth century.

As Jung looked at the world, the Christian religion, as it had been presented and lived to that point in Europe, was not adequate to contain the powerful splitting tendencies at work in history. It simply hid people's heads in the sand and foolishly let them believe that everything would come out alright in the end since a good God is supposedly in control of history. For Jung, the example of Jesus Christ taught the opposite—the image of the wholly good God is shattered by betrayal on the cross and ends in tragedy. People have to grow up and take responsibility for history and for the planet and not wait passively for a good God to put things right. One must take a less naïve view of God. This is the fiercely delivered message of his *Answer to Job*.

CONCLUSION

I believe that Victor White achieved wisdom and did not fall into cynicism as a result of his betrayal at the hands of Jung. In the end he was able to see Jung's person more clearly, for better and for worse, without casting him utterly aside. The transference object was broken and a new consciousness had space to dawn in him. In a final exchange of letters shortly before White's death from inoperable cancer in 1960, both men showed gratitude for what they had learned from the other. They had separated but had not become antagonists or enemies. They overcame splitting in favor of holding together the opposites and achieving object wholeness. This is the psychological basis of wisdom.

I will close with a story that for me illustrates so well the passage from betrayal through darkness to wisdom.

> By the time he was fifteen, Elie Wiesel was in Auschwitz . . . [where a] teacher of Talmud befriended him. . . .
>
> One night the teacher took Wiesel back to his own barracks, and there, with the young boy as the only witness, three great Jewish scholars—masters of Talmud, Halakhah, and Jewish jurisprudence—put God on trial, creating, in that eerie place, "a rabbinic court of law to indict the Almighty." The trial lasted several nights. Witnesses were heard, evidence was gathered, conclusions were drawn, all of which issued finally in a unanimous verdict: the Lord God Almighty, Creator of Heaven and Earth, was found *guilty* of crimes against creation and humankind. And then, after what Wiesel describes as an "infinity of silence," the Talmudic scholar looked at the sky and said "It's time for evening prayers," and the members of the tribunal recited Maariv, the evening service.[14]

God may be guilty, unreliable, unfathomable, but God is still God, and it is better to recognize that reality than to turn one's back on truth or ignore it. This is the beginning of wisdom, or so it seems to me.

NOTES

[1] Job 28:12. All quotations from the Bible are from the Revised Standard Version.

[2] Deuteronomy 7:12–14.

[3] C. G. Jung, *Answer to Job*, in *Psychology and Religion: West and East*, vol. 11 of *The Collected Works of C. G. Jung*, ed. Herbert Read, Michael Fordham, and Gerhard Adler, trans. R. F. C. Hull (Princeton, N.J.: Princeton University Press, 1952).

[4] Job 19: 25–27.

[5] See Michael Fordham, *Jungian Psychotherapy: A Study in Analytical Psychology* (New York: John Wiley and Sons, 1978), p. 92.

[6] Victor White quoted in *The Jung-White Letters,* ed. Anne Conrad Lammers and Adrian Cunningham, contributing ed. Murray Stein (London: Routledge, 2005), p. 254n6.

[7] White to Jung, 17 March 1955, in *ibid.,* p. 259.

[8] Donald Kalsched, *The Inner World of Trauma: Archetypal Defences of the Personal Spirit* (London: Routledge, 1996).

[9] See Murray Stein, *Jung's Treatment of Christianity: The Psychotherapy of a Religious Tradition* (Wilmette, Ill.: Chiron Publications, 1985).

[10] *The Jung-White Letters: A Theatrical Performance and Discussion,* available on DVD from The Asheville Jung Center (http://ashevillejungcenter.org).

[11] White to Jung, 17 March 1955, in *The Jung-White Letters,* p. 259.

[12] *Ibid.*

[13] Jung to White, 2 April 1955, in *ibid.,* p. 261.

[14] Robert McAffee Brown, "Introduction," in Elie Wiesel, *The Trial of God (as It Was Held on February 25, 1649, in Shamgorod): A Play in Three Acts* (1979; repr., New York: Schocken, 1995), p. vii. Brown's italics.

2

Betrayal of the Self, Self-Betrayal, and the Leap of Trust: The Book of Job, a Tale of Individuation

Diane Cousineau Brutsche

Whether brutal and dramatic or subtle and inconspicuous, experiences of betrayal are multifaceted and belong to the history of most (if not all) individuals. Stories of betrayal abound in literature and films. They are also found in myths and fairy tales originating from all cultures, an affirmation of the archetypal dimension of the reality of betrayal.

THE BOOK OF JOB: AN ARCHETYPAL STORY OF BETRAYAL

Using the mythological text of the Old Testament, the book of Job, I will explore the archetypal root of individual experiences of betrayal and show how this mythological story can point the way toward the development of trust and self-trust.

The book of Job is one of the major texts (if not the most explicit one) in the Judeo-Christian literature to highlight the ambivalent nature of the Divine; that is, the oneness of the creative and destructive principles within the Divine archetype, or that which we normally identify from a human perspective as Good and Evil. It gave birth to Jung's monograph *Answer to Job*, a powerful and emotionally charged text in which Jung concentrated on the relationship between Job, Yahweh, and Satan, which he understood to be archetypal images of the Ego, the Self, and the dark side of the Self.[1] Despite the impressive quality of Jung's interpretation, he overlooked the Bible's staging of several other characters who play crucial roles in Job's process and bring a very different meaning to the story than the one Jung extracted from it.

If we approach the text as an expression of an intrapsychic process, not only can Yahweh be seen as a personification of the Self (as Jung pointed out) and Job as a personification of the Ego, but all the other characters that are mentioned can symbolize different parts of Job's psyche: anima, shadow, complexes, and so forth. When the text is explored in this wider intrapsychic perspective, it becomes vibrant with life and very close to our human experiences.

THE INITIAL SITUATION

The story begins in the tone of a fairy tale:

> There was once a man in the land of Uz whose name was Job. That man was blameless and upright, one who feared God and turned away from evil. There were born to him seven sons and three daughters. He had seven thousand sheep, three thousand camels, five hundred yoke of oxen, five hundred donkeys, and very many servants; so that this man was the greatest of all the people of the east.[2]

In this first passage, Job is presented as a faithful, blameless servant of God; he has many children and enjoys wealth and reputation. He seems blessed by God, one who is in God's good graces. We also have here a perfect symbolic description of a well-developed Ego that has acquired a large number of qualities—an abundance of psychic resources that are at its disposal—and has reached the zenith of its power. Such a state corresponds precisely to what Jung describes as the fulfillment of the task of the Ego during the first half of life.[3] Nothing in this description seems to forebode tragedy. Nothing, that is, except for a few important symbolic details. First, what is very noticeable is that there is no mention whatsoever of Job's wife. Job represents a well-developed masculine consciousness but one that is still incomplete, one that does not have an integrated feminine dimension in symbolic correspondence with Yahweh, one that is presented in the text as a one-sided patriarchal God-image. In the text, after these first few lines about Job himself, we are given some information about his children and how he reacts to their behavior.

> His sons used to go and hold feasts in one another's houses in turn; and they would send and invite their three sisters to eat and drink with them. And when the feast days had run their course, Job would send and sanctify them, and he would rise early in the morning and offer burned offerings according to the number of them all; for Job said, "It may be that my children

have sinned, and cursed God in their hearts." This is what Job always did.[4]

This passage is most interesting from a psychological point of view, particularly regarding the theme of trust. Symbolically, Job's children can represent qualities of the psyche that are still not fully developed (younger parts of the psyche). But I would also be tempted to interpret them as elements of the shadow since they appear as energies that are completely opposite to Job's conscious choice of incarnating "saintliness." They feast, they eat and drink. In other words, they manifest as Dionysian parts of the psyche, contrasting strongly with Job's seemingly more ascetic lifestyle. Moreover they exist separated from the Ego, living in their own house and having their feasts away from Job's sight, away from the Ego's consciousness.

Even though he does not witness his children's feasts directly, Job obviously distrusts these shadow energies. His attempts to atone for their potential sins show how threatened he feels by these unconscious impulses and consequently how he is compelled to suppress them. His repetitive rituals of atonement also prove his distrust of Yahweh. Despite the fact that he has been generously blessed by Yahweh in all aspects of his life, Job lives in fear of his God's wrath should his own shadow ever be activated. Genuine, mature trust in himself, in his Father, in life in general is therefore not yet a reality in Job's psyche. In spite of a successful Ego development, he remains spiritually immature, living his relationship with God like a frightened child, still imprisoned in a world of rules and conditional love. Needless to say, if the individual's psyche is to access its full potential and authenticity, a radical inner movement has to be initiated to free the psyche from this state of fear.

THE BETRAYAL

Depth psychology teaches that any psychic energy that is strongly repressed on the conscious level tends to manifest dramatically in the unconscious, following the law of compensation. And indeed this is what happens in Job's life. One day, Satan presents himself to the heavenly realm and Yahweh welcomes him, even engaging in a conversation with him. When Satan suggests putting Job's devotion to a trial, Yahweh agrees (after a few weak hesitations) to deliver Job into Satan's hands. Immediately afterward, a whole series of misfortunes descend upon Job. His servants are killed, his cattle are stolen by hordes of enemies or burned by a fire falling from heaven, his children are killed as the house where they were feasting collapses, and finally he is stricken by a terrible illness; and all this without any justification, without any fault on the part of Job that could have raised God's wrath.

The Shattered Psyche

Having been so brutally betrayed by his divine Father, having lost everything including his physical health, Job finds himself in a state of material and spiritual misery, feeling completely bewildered and helpless. Then, says the text, Job "took a potsherd with which to scrape himself, and sat among the ashes."[5]

As soon as they hear of his misfortunes, his three friends come and sit by his side. None of them can utter a single word. The whole Ego realm is defeated and reduced to absolute numbness. Job is stripped of all of his energies. Symbolically speaking, all his inner resources have fallen into the depths of the unconscious, leaving the Ego in a state of deep regression, a typical post-traumatic state.

The period of numbness lasts seven days and seven nights, a full "organic" cycle. The betrayed psyche is wounded beyond words, and it is only after a long period of muteness that Job begins to retrieve his speech. But all he can utter are death wishes. He wishes that he had never been born[6] or that he had died at birth[7] or that death would come and take him now.[8] In this extreme state of regression, Job can express nothing but his wish for self-annihilation. Yet as defeatist as it may sound, it is a totally genuine and courageous expression of his inner state. Without this act of courage, no healing process can unfold.

Indeed, as the text shows, as soon as Job comes out of his silence, the voices of his friends also start to make themselves heard. Psychic energies are set in motion again. The Ego can then start dealing with its traumatic experience instead of merely enduring it passively.

The Activation of the Complexes

Surrounded by his three friends, Job begins to try to make sense of his cruel experience. Biblical commentators usually refer to Job's friends as "the comforters." As representations of an intrapsychic reality, I propose that we see them as "complexes"; that is, clusters of energies or subpersonalities that belong to Job's psyche. Complexes are essentially related to emotions, and they get constellated automatically when the Ego experiences a situation that raises emotion. Needless to say, after a betrayal, the emotional situation is extreme, so the complexes are powerfully constellated.

What follows is a long struggle between Job and his friends (between the Ego and the complexes) to come to terms with the situation, a dialogue in which the so-called comforters begin to manifest in a way that is anything but comforting. All through these long chapters the "comforters" act exactly as complexes do, giving voice to a whole set of neurotic defenses that one finds in a post-traumatic state: denial, self-blame, idealization of the betrayer, and rationalizations of all sorts, all aimed at avoiding the realization of the painful reality while keeping the psyche neurotically bound with the betrayer. This process leads to self-betrayal, a very insidious defense mechanism that can often last for a whole lifetime, keeping an individual estranged from his or her true self.

Here are a few examples of the comforters' arguments: "Is not your fear of God your confidence," says one of Job's friends, "and the integrity of your ways your hope?"[9] (Denial.) Another says, "As I have seen, those who plow iniquity and sow trouble reap the same."[10] (Self-blame.) Another asks, "Does God pervert justice? Or does the Almighty pervert the right?"[11] (Idealization of the betrayer.)

Complexes dwell in a realm that is very different from the realm of the Ego. They draw their emotional energy from past experiences and have no part in events happening on the conscious level. They are much too immersed in unconscious contents to be able to deal with any of the differentiation that can take place only on the conscious level. They function like a tape recorder, repeating again and again the same old recorded messages. And whenever they come closer to consciousness, a bit less immersed in the unconscious thanks to the Ego's effort to engage in a dialogue with them, they tend to remain bound to the collective consciousness. So Job's friends remain locked in their motionless world and keep looking for sins he might have committed that would have raised God's wrath. They ask him to repent in order to regain God's favor. They keep plaguing him, repeating over and over again the same conventional "words of wisdom" that correspond to the voice of the collective consciousness.

As the dialogue progresses, however, Job begins to realize that the multiple tragedies that have descended upon him have nothing to do with faults of his own. They are genuine "acts of God," the acts of an unpredictable divine energy, tragedies that no human fault can justify. He has directly witnessed the untrustworthy, ruthless nature of his divine Father, a set of events that contradicts completely his previous perspective of Yahweh as an all-good, loving, and just Father. But each of his efforts to express this nascent awareness encounters his friends' rebukes. They go on blaming him, even if they cannot concretely name any of the many sins they suppose he has committed.

While complexes are not innovative, they are very stubborn. Nevertheless they play an important role in the process of individuation and in the healing of a betrayal wound, provided that the Ego gathers the strength to bear the tension that their activity necessarily generates. As a disharmony progressively sets in between a new Ego experience and the repetitive messages of the complexes, the Ego finds itself forced to take a stand of its own and bear witness to the new reality that demands to be integrated. As his voice gains strength, Job becomes increasingly angry toward his friends and irritated by their boring and useless speeches. A creative inner conflict arises.

"My companions are treacherous," says Job. "In time of heat they disappear. . . . Such you have now become to me; you see my calamity and are afraid."[12] The distance he is setting between himself and his friends allows him to gain a fundamental insight into the dynamics they respond to. He now perceives the grounds on which their rationalizations rest: fear of facing the unknown, fear of the overwhelming and unpredictable power of whatever rules human fate. If fear is what keeps one bound to a neurotic state, the way out can only be through confronting the fear. And this is what Job does.

Not only does he confront his friends but he also turns toward Yahweh himself and expresses his anger against him. "I will not restrain my mouth. . . . I will complain in the bitterness of my soul. . . . What are human beings . . . that you set your mind on them? . . . If I sin, what do I do to you, you watcher of humanity? . . . Does it seem good to you to oppress?"[13] One can see that Job has grown from the frightened and obedient child of God that he was into an adult who speaks his own mind in spite of the huge risk involved.

Of course such words trigger even stronger reactions from Job's friends. "How long will you say these things?" says one of them. "Inquire now of bygone generations, and consider what their ancestors have found. . . . Will they not teach you and tell you and utter words out of their understanding?"[14] This of course means, "How dare you step off the beaten paths? Who do you think you are to question the wisdom of your ancestors?"

By now, however, the emotional symbiosis between the Ego and the complexes is broken and the Ego is impermeable to their arguments. So

Job continues to confront his friends and Yahweh. "As for you," says he to his friends, "you whitewash with lies; all of you are worthless physicians."[15] "Your maxims are proverbs of ashes," he says, "your defenses are defenses of clay. Let me have silence and I will speak, and let come on me what may. . . . See, he will kill me; I have no hope; but I will defend my ways to his face."[16] And again, "As long as my breath is in me . . . my lips will not speak falsehood. . . . Far be it from me to say that you are right; until I die I will not put my integrity from me."[17]

Job has overcome his fear of Yahweh, his fear of death. From now on he is ready to die, ready to be crushed by the Almighty rather than betray his own truth. This readiness to die is completely different from the death wishes Job had previously expressed. A death wish is a resignation to hopelessness. A readiness to die, in contrast, is a powerful affirmation of one's readiness to live genuinely. Self-betrayal has come to an end. Finally, after this interminable struggle, it is said: "So these three men ceased to answer Job, because he was righteous in his own eyes."[18] The Ego has done its task. The complexes are reduced to silence. The rest of the process will have to unfold from another dimension.

THE LEAP OF TRUST

What makes an experience of betrayal potentially deeply transformative is the fact that genuine, mature trust cannot be found again on the level where the betrayal has taken place. On that level one would remain fixated in what Jung calls "neurotic suffering," either imprisoned in a cynical attitude and protecting oneself against further betrayal by refusing to trust anymore or attributing the painful experience to the individual person of the betrayer and naïvely continuing to idealize potential future relationships at the risk of falling repeatedly into the victim role. Trust in its deepest meaning must be searched for beyond the personal level; it requires a leap beyond rationality, toward an awareness of the coexistence of both light and darkness in any reality and a willingness to embrace both at once. This attitude is the key to the activation of what is called in Jungian terms the "transcendent function," itself giving access to the "unifying symbol"; that is, the third realm of reality that emerges from the tension of the opposites. This level of consciousness characterizes a psyche that has attained its full maturity.[19]

No ready-made formula exists that would allow a human psyche to gain access to this other level of consciousness. The soul, however, is constantly giving hints of the direction to follow. Even in the darkest moments following an experience of betrayal, a voice from a deeper layer of the psyche may be heard that expresses healing intuitions. In Job's story, for instance, even at a moment when on the conscious level he could not yet express anything other than death wishes, a voice that the text attributed to God spoke within him, heralding the revelation of a new perspective: "Do not despise the discipline of the Almighty. For he wounds, but he binds up; he strikes, but his hands heal."[20] In a moment of such distress, this nascent paradoxical perspective reaches the conscious Ego more like a whisper than a statement and could in many cases pass unnoticed. If heard, however, and not rejected it creates an opening for the emergence of the transcendent function. This is what will allow Job to begin wishing for the manifestation of the benevolent side of God: "I must appeal for mercy to my accuser."[21] Later we hear him say: "There is no umpire [mediator] between us, who might lay his hand on us both."[22] This sentence comes out like a sigh, "If only there would be a mediator!"

But even if the presence of the mediator is not yet perceptible, the longing for it is already there. Such longings in the midst of distress are spontaneous acts of the creative imagination, and as soon as they find expression, the reality they evoke is in the process of being constellated. They are like seeds planted in the psyche that will later grow and bear fruit. They are what will eventually enable Job to affirm: "I know that my redeemer lives and that at the end he will stand upon the earth."[23] Such a powerful affirmation is not a denial of the ruthless side of Yahweh and a blind attempt to cling to a one-sided view of an all-loving, benevolent Father. Job's psyche has reached the point where the separation between light and darkness has been overcome. Job's soul is ripe for his reconciliation with the almighty power that rules over human destinies.

"I know that you can do all things," says he to Yahweh finally, "and that no purpose of yours can be thwarted. . . . I have uttered what I did not understand, things too wonderful for me which I did not know. . . . I had heard of you by the hearing of the ear, but now my eye sees you; therefore I despise myself, and repent in dust and ashes."[24]

The God Job is bowing before is no longer the one he was previously trying to appease with his rituals of atonement or one whom he would now try to appease by a feigned humility. Job is bowing before the cosmic unpredictable power and courageously embracing it, whatever it may bring. He does not demand anything from it; he simply acknowledges the infinite distance between his human dimension and the incomprehensible "phenomenon" of a divine creative and destructive energy. Job is humbled but not humiliated: having stood truthful to himself in spite of the risk of being annihilated, having embodied the only power a human being can have, he can now acknowledge his powerlessness without loss of his dignity.

Such a surrender of all expectations without surrender of one's dignity and without denial of one's soul needs reveals itself as the key that opens the door toward healing. As much as wishes are natural and creative energies of the psyche, expectations, for their part, are like attempts to impose one's desires on life. Experience proves again and again that such an attitude "displeases" life, which seems to respond more willingly to a paradoxical attitude on the part of the Ego: the paradox of "affirmation/ surrender" all at once. Needless to say, such an attitude cannot be generated by the Ego. It can only come from the soul and from the Ego's willingness to obey its voice.

Immediately after Job's soulful surrender, Yahweh's benevolence is constellated again. Job's children are given back to him: the creative potentials that had sunk into the unconscious and had been split off from the Ego are retrieved. Furthermore, Yahweh reinstates Job's fortune severalfold: the psyche is not only restored to its previous state but is enlarged, magnified. Job's breakdown has resulted in what James Hillman has called "a breakthrough onto another level of consciousness,"[25] where a lasting trust can be experienced, one that includes the risk of a renewed betrayal, one that does not shy at the dark side of reality but embraces it. Such an unconditional acceptance of reality widens the inner space and allows the psyche to unfold freely its full potential. This is the goal and meaning of a working through of a betrayal.

JOB AND THE HUMAN REALITY OF BETRAYAL

Job's story provides us with an archetypal pattern underlying the human reality of betrayal and trust. Those who have been the victims of a brutal trauma (child abuse, rape, earthquake, war, etc.) will probably have no difficulty indentifying with Job's excruciating pain and his struggle to come to terms with his experience. But the story is valuable even for those who have not experienced such extreme circumstances. Betrayal indeed can sometimes come in very inconspicuous guises, and because of this insidious quality, the experience may remain forever out of reach of consciousness, leaving the individual "blind to betrayal,"[26] in Jennifer Freyd's apt language, and condemned to a life of unconscious self-betrayal.

The perpetrator may even be what I would call a "benevolent betrayer": a parental figure, most of the time a personality that is too dominant, acting perhaps out of sincere good will but unfortunately out of his/her own inadequacies and insecurities that get projected onto the child. This leads to a surrender of the child's true self in exchange for love and recognition. Such a parental figure ends up betraying the child's soul, often without even realizing it.

This was the case of a former male analysand. His father had been a very successful man and a powerful personality whom the entire family had put on a pedestal. The personality of the father was still hovering over the family eight years after he had died. What had prompted the analysand to come to me were increasing symptoms of depression and self-sabotage as well as a puzzling series of recurrent dreams, all of them revolving around his father's unfinished burial. He was finding himself at the funeral home where his father's corpse was still breathing or in the cemetery carrying the father's body in a hearse and desperately looking for a place to bury him without ever finding it, or he was trying to put the corpse in a coffin that always proved to be too small, and so forth and so on.

Through our sessions it became obvious that he had transformed his father into a God image, someone he had always been trying to imitate without of course ever completely succeeding, desperately trying, in his own words, "to be a good photocopy rather than a bad original." I cannot think of a more accurate expression to describe what self-betrayal is about. As he progressively became aware of his imprisonment in the father's image, he started asking himself how he could finally bury his father. This question led him to realize that it would be impossible to bury his father as long as his father's image remained, as it did, so alive and powerful in his psyche. The "old king" needed to be killed for his son to access his full life energy. The process met with a lot of resistance. Behind each personal father lies the archetype, and this is why admitting the dark side of the father, even of a plainly human one, can almost feel like a blasphemy. The analysand's struggle took shapes that resembled Job's dialogue with his "comforters" before he could finally free himself as well as his memory of his father from their mutual imprisonment in the archetype.

Even if one is not confronted, as Job was, with Yahweh himself, one should not underestimate the courage it takes to heal a human betrayal. Betrayal invariably affects the psyche to its deepest roots. When it is made conscious, it is experienced as a threat to one's own being, and the path toward healing is paved with pain. The courage to trust is like the courage to be: it always has "the character of 'in spite of,'"[27] as Paul Tillich would say—that is, in spite of the constant threat that it will be shattered. Even in the most trustworthy relationship, the threat of death, the ultimate betrayer, is always present. This is what makes trust, in its profoundest quality, such a noble human endeavor.

NOTES

[1] C. G. Jung, *Answer to Job*, in *Psychology and Religion: West and East*, vol. 11 of *The Collected Works of C. G. Jung*, ed. Herbert Read, Michael Fordham, and Gerhard Adler, trans. R. F. C. Hull (Princeton, N.J.: Princeton University Press, 1952).

[2] Job 1:1–3. All quotations from the Bible are from the New Revised Standard Version.

[3] C. G. Jung, "The Stages of Life," in *Structure and Dynamics of the Psyche*, vol. 8 of *The Collected Works of C. G. Jung*, ed. and trans. Gerhard Adler and R. F. C. Hull (Princeton, N.J.: Princeton University Press, 1970), §§749–795.

[4] Job 1:4–5.

[5] Job 2:8.

[6] "Let the day perish in which I was born"; Job 3:3.

[7] "Why did I not die at birth, come forth from the womb and expire?"; Job 3:11.

[8] "Why is light given to one in misery, and life to the bitter in soul, who long for death, but it does not come?"; Job 3:20–21.

[9] Job 4:6.

[10] Job 4:8.

[11] Job 8:3.

[12] Job 6:15–17, 21.

[13] Job 7:11, 17, 20; Job 10:3.

[14] Job 8:2, 8, 10.

[15] Job 13:4.

[16] Job 13:12–15.

[17] Job 27:3–5.

[18] Job 32:1.

[19] See C. G. Jung, "The Transcendent Function," in *Structures and Dynamics of the Psyche*, vol. 8 of *The Collected Works of C. G. Jung*, ed. and trans. Gerhard Adler and R. F. C. Hull (Princeton, N.J.: Princeton University Press, 1970), §§131–193.

[20] Job 5:17–18.

[21] Job 9:15.

[22] Job 9:33.

[23] Job 19:25.

[24] Job 42:2, 5–6.

[25] James Hillman, "Betrayal," in *Loose Ends: Primary Papers in Analytical Psychology* (Dallas, Tex.: Spring Publications, 1975), p. 67.

[26] Jennifer J. Freyd, "Blind to Betrayal: New Perspectives on Memory for Trauma," *The Harvard Mental Health Letter* 15, no. 12 (1999): 4–6.

[27] Paul Tillich, *The Courage to Be* (New Haven, Conn.: Yale University Press, 1952), p. 4.

3

The Dawn of Religious Consciousness: Abraham, Isaac, and the Aqedah

John A. Desteian

INTRODUCTION

Since the theme of the 2010 Odyssey is trust and betrayal, it seemed reasonable to approach what Jews call the Aqedah, the binding of Isaac, by supposing that Abraham's trust in God was rewarded when God sent an angel to spare Isaac's life. Abraham's obedience and loyalty to God appear to have been the definitive qualities that saved Isaac from the immediate terrible fate that had earlier befallen Lot's wife. Adam and Eve, however, had already sealed the ultimate fate for the rest of humanity with a betrayal of their own. This is a conventional interpretation of the story, and it contributes, even today, to reverence for Abraham as the patriarchal progenitor of Judaism, Christianity, and Islam. The story of the Aqedah is an essential basis on which these religions have built their notions of trust, loyalty, submission, and betrayal (of god).

However, I take a different view. First, I see no reason to conceive this story as any truer an account of historical fact about a particular individual than any other fabulous tale in the Torah, the Bible, or the Koran. As a psychoanalyst interested in phenomenology, it is difficult to countenance the notion that this and other ancient stories can be misused to justify present-day political decisions and discord, even though such stories contained within them a political motivation from the very beginning. This leads me to a second point of departure. For me, the story exists as mythology, in the same way that accounts of Hermes' birth and Prometheus' gift of fire to mankind are. As mythology, the story has meaning

as a disclosing of a particularity of the human soul. But I encounter
Abraham's story as an ontological or, more properly, as a historico-
ontological record of human soul revealing itself to itself, a posteriori.

TRUST AND BETRAYAL

Before I get into a description of what I mean by a historico-ontological
record of soul-revealing, we need first to consider the existence of trust
and, by extension, betrayal. Many years ago, I wrote a little paper
challenging the rage of the moment, co-dependency. As part of the
discussion of the phenomenological difficulties of that strange social
movement, I had occasion to describe the problem the idea of trust
presents. I suggested that adult conceptions of trust don't actually exist as
such but exist only as a compromise. In discussing what happens in
interpersonal relations, I wrote:

> The passion of relationship becomes unconscious, and stability,
> predictability, and apparent security replace it, based on rules
> like, "I'll do this, and she'll do that." Following these rules results
> in "trust." Trust . . . however, may inhibit interaction. . . . Often,
> trust is an unconscious foreshortening of the phrase, "I trust
> that you will follow the explicit and implicit rules of our
> relationship, so I can avoid suffering." Whatever the underlying
> agreement . . . the longing to trust expresses the desire to become
> unconscious. It is the desire to let go of anxiety which requires
> humans to be alert. If we trust, we needn't pay attention. If we
> trust, we can fall asleep. Since humans are fallible, we are, by
> definition, untrustworthy. What happens when trust is
> breached? . . . [One says, by inference,] "I don't trust myself to
> know what to do in that situation." We place our anxiety in the
> hands of another person. Then, if we can manage them, we don't
> have to deal with our anxieties.[1]

It was apparent to me then, as it is now, that trust is the situation
infants and young children find themselves afflicted with, without self-
consciousness and thus instinctually, since they have no other recourse or
resource. Neither, we presume, do chimpanzees, birds, and most other
animals, until they are fully fledged. As babies, toddlers, and young children,
we certainly cannot rely on ourselves, so we live within and later introject
and reconstruct the useful illusion that our caregivers are trustworthy,
despite what we later come to know as empathic failures, disappointments,
and frustrations. As we grow up, we extend that same courtesy to our
teachers, religious leaders, friends, and lovers and, finally, to our analysts.

Only later do we discover, oftentimes with disastrous consequences, that no other person's interests, attitudes, morality, and desires run parallel to our own. In the analytic setting, "optimal frustration"[2] feels like betrayal, and it becomes something else, if it becomes anything at all, only after the fact, on reflection, and with considerable working through. Beyond a certain maturational point, trust requires us to suspend the kind of self-consciousness we now come equipped with, to one degree or another, and have developed throughout the ages since humans began to communicate in abstract form through such means as hieroglyphs and writing. That, to be sure, is a very long time. Yet suspension of self-consciousness is not possible. The persona, the mask we all present to the world to protect us from being harmed, is the most immediate evidence of the impossibility of suspending self-consciousness. It follows then that adult notions of trust exist for the sake of appearances only, to give an impression, whatever that impression is intended to convey, either consciously or unconsciously.

An analogous situation of trust and betrayal presents itself for our consideration if we turn our attention to religion. We have all heard stories of devoutly religious people turning away from a god who has betrayed their trust, for example by allowing their innocent child to be killed. Or we may recall Antonio Salieri in the film version of *Amadeus,* who denounces and damns a god who would create his humble servant with the ability to recognize but not compose beauty through music. Even though Salieri had faithfully and loyally submitted himself, God had cursed him with the fate of being compelled to stand by, to watch and listen while the irreverent Mozart made God's voice immanent through his music.

In these examples one can hear the simple, yet implicit, syllogism presented in the story of Abraham and Isaac, of trust and loyalty, of sacred covenant between god and the generations without end, the if-then that sits at the center of collective consciousness and the religious rituals performed throughout the millennia. Here we arrive at the beginning of the story of Abraham, not in Genesis 1, not in Genesis at all, but in a story many of us will have never heard, especially if we are Christians.

ABRAHAM THE IDOL-SMASHER

The story, for our purposes, is composed of three parts. The first involves Abraham, his father, and King Nimrod. In the Torah and the Christian Bible, there is little mention of Abraham's father beyond the bare fact that he came from a family of idol worshippers. A Midrash and the Koran present the idea that his father was an idol maker, while Genesis gives the lineage and says only that Abraham and his family were directed by God to leave the land of his father and establish an everlasting bond with Yahweh in Canaan. The Midrashim are said to be an exegesis on the oral tradition that accompanied but was not included in the written Torah, for which Moses was the scribe and God the narrator.[3] In accordance with belief in the magical properties of words, the early Jews forbade the saying or writing of certain words and ideas (for example the name Yahweh), and the oral tradition appears to have been consistent with this superstition. We need the oral tradition to fill in our knowledge of the stories from that ancient time. The Midrashim were not written down until the Middle Ages, and we might be suspicious that the contents of the Midrashim were actually expressions of latter-day revisionism assigned to an earlier time without the evidence provided in the Koran.[4] That text, which appeared in the seventh century of the Common Era, confirms the story of Abraham the idol-smasher. This concurrence suggests that the oral tradition about this story was widely known.

According to the oral tradition, Abraham's father, Terah, was not merely a worshipper of idols but also a maker of idols, an artisan who fashioned idols for worship. One day, while Terah was gone, several people came to purchase idols, and through his use of deft reasoning, Abraham was able to demonstrate the folly of idol worship. He smashed all the idols save one, the largest, and placed a stick in that idol's hand. When Terah returned and saw the smashed idols, he was distressed. Abraham told him that there had been a fight among the idols over an offering of flour and that the largest had taken the stick to the others for the sake of securing the flour for himself. The Midrash story says that Terah knew that Abraham's explanation was a mockery. From the distance of several millennia, we can say that Abraham demonstrated to Terah (and to all of us) that idols cannot act in the animated, physical world. Terah turned Abraham over to King Nimrod, but even the king was not successful in arguing the point with Abraham. First, Nimrod suggested that if idols had no power, surely fire did. But when Abraham said that water had power over fire, Nimrod suggested that water be worshipped. Abraham responded that water was absorbed by the clouds and dispersed by the wind, so Nimrod offered the wind as the object of worship.[5]

The story goes on from there to Abraham's punishment at Nimrod's hand and God saving him from fire, but that is of no consequence for our discussion. Consider the lawyerly brief Abraham presented to both his father's customers and to Nimrod, and his effectiveness. The rudiments of a modern syllogism were present in the story: If the god is in the object, then the gods may fight among themselves. If the god is not in the object, then the story that the gods fought among themselves is ridiculous. Then, in Genesis, Abraham learns of the imminent destruction of the towns of Sodom and Gomorrah and the people in them as punishment for their sinfulness.[6] Abraham asks God if He will spare the corrupt people of the cities if he, Abraham, can find 50, then 45, then 30, then 20, then 10 righteous people in the cities. At the mention of each figure, God offers a reprieve. Here also Abraham the lawyer shows his mettle. Abraham's argument is not the problem; his clients, the Sodomites and Gomorrans, are. Finally, the legend of Abraham and Isaac that we find at Genesis 22 can come into view. "After these things," which is now translated as "some 'time' later," God tells Abraham to take his son Isaac to a particular place and sacrifice him as a burnt offering. (Phrases such as "after these things" were the stimuli for or are indications of Midrash stories, which filled in the blanks with the oral tradition.) Abraham, ever obedient to Yahweh, submits and sets out with his son. When God sees that Abraham has proven his devotion by offering his son as a sacrifice, he lets them both off the hook and a ram appears to be sacrificed in lieu of the son.

MYTHICAL CONSCIOUSNESS

Two questions arise as we now consider these stories. First, does the idea "smashing of idols" indicate anything of significance to us today, in relation to *participation mystique*? I am not discussing iconoclasm here, the destruction of icons, but something more originary, fundamental, and formal. Second, of equal importance, what do the stories inscribe of the movement of the human soul? While these seem to be two different questions, they are actually the same one in different forms.

The idol-smashing Abraham presents us with the unasked question What is god? That is, it problematizes god. It brings into the open an episteme that reasons from appearances—that is, empirically. Implicit in the narrative is an acknowledgment that once upon a time, the living god was in an object, was the object. The idol or statue was not a mere representation, re-presentation, of god, a reflection of god whose residence is elsewhere. The idol was no less god and no less life- and fate-determining than a termite mound or a chicken oracle to the Azande or a fetish object might be to someone with a modern sexual compulsion.[7]

What does it mean to problematize something? When something is problematized, our attention is drawn to elements of that something that appear as troublesome or difficult. Through this process we consider its existence, ontologically, epistemologically, and hermeneutically. Consider a hammer. It clearly exists. We know it empirically: we can see it, touch it, feel its heft, and so forth. We can weigh it, put it under a microscope, or burn or melt it to determine its composition. The hammer is, accordingly, ready-to-hand, to borrow a concept from Martin Heidegger. We don't think about the hammer at all, even when we pick it up to use it to pound a nail into a board. But if we pick up that same hammer and notice that its head is loose, the hammer is problematized. It becomes, again using Heidegger's term, present-at-hand. We become conscious of the hammer as something, a hammer, and also as something it is not, a hammer we can use safely. What appears in that moment is difference.

The problematic of a material and mechanistic hammer is easily resolved. But what about some "thing" that is not of the material or mechanical world—truth, for example, or being? Or god? The brief Midrash story of Abraham the idol-smasher indicates the problematization of god, but not a particular god—Yahweh, for example, or Nimrod's fire god or Baal or the Zoroastrian Ahura Mazda or the Hindu Agni. Rather, the story indicates the problematizing of what constitutes god. The reasoning that Abraham used with his father regarding the idols and with God in relation to the destruction of Sodom and Gomorrah indicated the interiorization of the notion of god that originated in an empirical, reasoned epistemology. Another way to say that is this: the notion of god became known to consciousness as the notion of god. God became a notion as a construction of empirical human experience. For many millennia, gods and human experience were an undifferentiated unity. In prehistory, god didn't exist for humans in any form in which actions of humans and the world could be discreetly differentiated. Ernst Cassirer wrote:

> What is commonly called the sensory consciousness [empirical consciousness, the content of the world of "perception"] . . . is a product of abstraction, a theoretical elaboration of the "given." Before self-consciousness rises to this abstraction, it lives in the world of the mythical consciousness, a world not of "things" and their "attributes" but of mythical potencies and powers, of demons and gods. . . . Science arose in and worked itself out of the sphere of mythical immediacy.[8]

Mythical consciousness *predated* magic, occult substances, nonmechanical relations, angels, demons, gods, and all other notions (abstractions) that gave meaning to appearances within the world. Mythical consciousness predated the beginning of making meaning of phenomena, hermeneutics. In mythical consciousness, the world does not exist for humans any more than water does for fish. The abstraction that is the world cannot be created before the world exists as an abstraction, and it cannot have an abstract creator until the world as having been created has been created as an abstraction. And it cannot be recorded abstractly until recording has been abstractly conceived. When we consider the story of Abraham, we are witnessing a much later moment than mythical consciousness. It is, rather, religious consciousness, a conscious realization of god as god, as some presence that has a life separate from that of which nature is constituted. Of course, we are not actually witnessing it, since its having been written already indicates the form of consciousness that would permit something to be written in the first instance. We are actually reading a historical account, a historico-ontological account of an elastic stage in the development of human consciousness in narrative, imaginal form collapsed into and re-presented as a moment. We are presented with a soul looking back on itself as a constituent of its own history. What has become for modernity the "logical constitution of consciousness"[9] and with it the constitution of our scientific knowledge and epistemology shows itself in its infancy in the story of Abraham, the idol-smashing barrister-in-chief.

We can consider even further this "moment" that is not a moment: it is an event of ontology in which the thing, the idol, appears for itself as a "thing," not a "being." It is also an event of epistemology. The thing, the idol, appears for itself as a thing, a piece of wood or stone, by virtue of the use of reasoning of "if . . . then." In addition, it is a hermeneutic event, where the already posited meaning of the "being" (idol) is negated, drained of its substance as "being," and by virtue of that negation is posited as some "other" thing. The thing ceases to exist as *that* thing, god, and becomes in its place *another* thing, a representation of god, a reenactment of an earlier, mythic form of consciousness that has been negated.

But of course not entirely negated, even though god was no longer things—fire, water, mountains, trees, statuary, and so forth. According to the story, god was now present, posited as voice, as idea, as morality, as word. God became abstract, an abstraction from "god = nature" to god as creator of nature and creator by virtue of the word, and we know that words signify difference. To think of Genesis as if it were an accurate historical account of events occurring sequentially from creation onward in time is to miss the potential symbolic meaning for consciousness within it. In the biblical beginning there was a void, and in the void darkness, which we now know to be the void and darkness in which no beginning could yet be thought or considered consciously, where time had no abstract relevance. When god said, "Let there be light" and there was light, the beginning, creation, had already become an abstract consequence of the development of the form of consciousness that the stories of Abraham symbolized. Even though Abraham's acts appear only later in the text, as if they took place after creation, they were actually a necessary precursor of the notion of a god of creation.

ABRAHAM, ISAAC, AND THE AQEDAH

We can now approach the Aqedah. It is worth noting that this event is not the sacrifice of the son, although Christians call it that and see in it the prefiguration of the crucifixion of Jesus as the messiah. Another inaccuracy is that Isaac is often imagined as a small child. But in the story Abraham burdened Isaac with the bundle of wood he had collected for the sacrificial act, and it is clear that if Isaac could carry the wood, he was not a small child. It also has been thought that the story symbolizes the end of child sacrifice, but this appears not to be so.[10] For psychoanalyst Silvano Arieti, the encounter between Abraham and God as it related to the sacrifice of Isaac represented the advent of self-conscious realization of morality.[11] I don't think Arieti is entirely inaccurate in this regard, but we humans couldn't become moral beings until something else occurred first. That "something" was the conscious realization of ourselves as children of god and thus children of an *idea*. We can call this reflexivity and reflectivity.

The concepts of god, idea, and morality are all equivalent in one way or another, like the three-faced goddess of the Greeks. We became reflexively to ourselves creatures of a creator, and only with the conception of creation could there come a conception of universal design. Archeologists tell us that the statuary and funerary activities of prehistoric human beings suggest that they were aware that they had been created. Of course, in the absence of written documentation, we are left with interpretation of the meaning of the archeological record. Nothing in that record suggests a conscious realization of a relationship between the idea of a creator and the idea of a creature. Rather, it appears to support the theory that an undifferentiated unity existed, a state of non-ideational consciousness that is for the most part beyond our capacity to imagine. If we imagine we are creatures of a creator, we do so self-consciously. We bring ourselves into ideal form, we are an idea of our own making, we are both subject and object. As a consequence the ideal form, ourselves as subject and object, negates the value of the imagining as an experience of undifferentiated unity.

Perhaps a crude analogue to the dim light of early primordial consciousness might be what we impute of how elephants experience death. These animals remain, often in an agitated state, around a dying or dead elephant and visit the places where the bones of dead relatives rest. These behaviors have been likened to the burial rituals of early humans.[12] The remnants, but only the remnants, of this mode of being are found in ancestor worship and similar rituals. Just as we wouldn't expect an elephant to explain, much less understand its ritual (repetitive) behavior, so we would refrain from asking an early human to describe what he or she was doing during rituals. As Jung said about the Pueblo sunrise ritual, it is done because it is done and has always been done so and without it the sun would not rise.[13]

If we are accurate in our interpretation of the legend of Abraham the idol-smasher, then, we humans have come to know ourselves as fully exposed to a world both benign and dangerous. To continue the metaphor I mentioned earlier, the fish had become aware of the water they were swimming in. But of course the world was not different by virtue of this realization. The world was only as benign and as dangerous after the development of consciousness as it had been before. After the development, humans saw idols as representing the gods located elsewhere, and in the gods were the cause of the bounty, potentiality, and dangers of the world. They were thought to be the cause of the fire of both the hearth and the conflagration, the water of both life and the flood, the wind that both propagated seeds and brought devastation. Centuries later, when another shift took place and these understandings were destroyed by the light of a form of conscious reasoning and empirical observation, the bounty, potentiality, and danger of the world still remained unchanged. What was changed was not the world but the *perception* of the world. What was changed was not the fact of being-in-the-world-fully-exposed, but the conscious and not yet entirely self-conscious *realization* that one was in the world and fully exposed to its dangers. And, more important, that one was equally exposed to both its bounty and its possibilities. Thus, the idea contained in the story of Abraham the idol-smasher discloses the working out of the problematization of one's exposure to the world, a new awareness that was conscious and yet not fully self-conscious.

If the story of idol-smashing Abraham represents the beginning by which the beginning could be told, then the binding of Isaac represents another decisive moment—once again, not a real moment, but the memory of a historical event of consciousness. In this moment, the Aqedah story symbolizes humankind's move out of one darkness, of mythic consciousness, and into a different darkness, religious consciousness, a darkness of soul-created, constructed meaning, of syllogistic ifs and thens: if I am a loyal and devoted servant of god, if I submit to the covenant I have been obedient to, then I will be . . .

The Isaac and Abraham who were saved from the sacrifice symbolize creatures of a creator. If we were to interpret the story as a modern narrative, we might expect that the child would end up being sacrificed, that our childish longings to belong and be protected and taken care of would need to be sacrificed, given up, let go of. Yet we know that this is not the case. Religious belief systems and the complaints of our analysands about betrayals of trust in adulthood show us something different. We still long for that belonging and protection.

The binding of Isaac represents the negation of the negation. First, in the story of Abraham the idol-smasher, undifferentiated unity was lost (negated), and with that negation appeared consciousness. It was not a foregone or necessary conclusion that consciousness would develop as a religious form. But it did. Religious consciousness was the form by which the void was filled as consciousness displaced undifferentiated unconsciousness. Collective (mass/group/tribe/sect) religious consciousness brought with it collective(mass/group/tribe/sect) unconsciousness, the negation of the negation. Abraham's idol-smashing and negotiating symbolize negation of an undifferentiated unity of consciousness and the world. Abraham's willingness to sacrifice his son symbolized the religious consciousness within which humankind sought safety. In his obedience to the demand that he sacrifice his son, the destructive world was still and always as it had been, but in the guise of Yahweh rather than fire, wind, or water. By submitting to God's command, both Abraham and Isaac represent the status of creatures of a creator, and with that status came the covenantal notion of continuity and salvation that *concealed* being-in-the-world-fully-exposed. Collective consciousness found its security and a modicum of serenity in the notion of God. Obedience to the word of God, the voice of God, seemed to promise a *secure* establishment and continuity of being, for the future. We only have to think about the belief that homosexuality or other behaviors that some consider to be immoral brought about Hurricane Katrina or the earthquake in Haiti or the 9/11 attacks to recognize the echo of Abraham's covenant. Bad things happen to bad people. If you are bad, then you will die.

The establishment and continuity of being now and in the future depends on obedience to God. Abraham and Isaac, symbolizing humankind as creatures of a creator, submitted to the status of children. In return, humankind was given the notions of both continuity and salvation that concealed the state of being-in-the-world-fully-exposed. Collective (religious/mass/group/tribe/sect) consciousness found its security and a modicum of serenity in the notion of god. However, at that time, the consequence of obedience to the covenant was not a prediction, but a foretelling, revelation. The state of being-in-the-world-fully-exposed was concealed within the comforting reassurance of foreknowledge, of revelation of the consequences of obedience to the covenant, taking on the quality of collective unconsciousness. The incipient if . . . then reasoning took this form: "If we submit to the word of God, if we accept our status as children, as creatures of the supraordinate creator, as moral beings, then we will be secure. If we are obedient to the will of God, then God will protect us"—and later, as empirical experience showed the inaccuracy of the first syllogism, "if not in this world, then in the next." What could better exemplify the notion of trust than this syllogism? And what could more explicitly indicate the shift in the locus of responsibility and freedom from ourselves to a protective and protecting Other? We humans emerged from our undifferentiated unity with the world into the world and knew our "fear and trembling" as a consequence of that emergence. We encountered a different way of knowing the world, as the stories tell us: through consciousness of darkness, the void, the abyss, and chaos. Just as we humans fortified ourselves against these threats physically, organizing ourselves into clans and tribes and towns, so also did we fortify ourselves emotionally—without reflexively knowing that we did so—with the notion of being creatures of a creator, a creator with whom we could come to negotiate a trusting relationship. And this fortification was a form of collective active imagination.

CONCLUSION

If we were to interpret the foregoing as criticism of the positing of god, god who appears as an abstraction, we would be interjecting a condemnation. Condemnation conceals the coming to know, retrospectively, in hindsight, the movements of consciousness—soul revealing itself to itself—as it has wended its way, metaphorically, into the form we now find ourselves both contained within and capable of observing. With our capability to observe the developments of consciousness it is as if we do so from the outside. But it is consciousness observing itself. Thus, we cannot know the movements of consciousness but only come to know, posit, self-consciously aware that what we posit is subject to contradiction and negation. Yet coming to know appears more open to the possibility of soul revealing itself than condemnation. And so if we were an advertising agency we might crudely understand and introduce the production thus: modern consciousness brought to you by religious consciousness. Religious consciousness itself has been (logically) and is being (practically) negated by empiricism, a scientific knowledge that has thrown the spotlight on magic and destroyed the occult substances. Religious consciousness, as such, has died of its success.

NOTES

[1] John Desteian, "Another Look at Co-Dependency," in *The Soul of Popular Culture: Looking at Contemporary Heroes, Myths, and Monsters,* ed. Mary Lynn Kittelson (Chicago: Open Court, 1998), p. 240.

[2] Heinz Kohut, *The Kohut Seminars on Self Psychology and Psychotherapy with Adolescents and Young Adults,* ed. Miriam Elson (New York: Norton, 1987), p. 92.

[3] "Just as the Written Law given by Moses emanates from God, whilst He Himself only proclaimed the first two commandments of the Decalogue, owing to the Israelites being too terrified to hear God's voice (Deuteronomy 20:19), and the whole of the Torah was then conveyed to Israel by Moses, so he likewise received the Oral law, which he was not allowed to commit to writing. This Oral law had to be taught by word of mouth side by side with the Written law, and thus the former became an unfolding and sequel to the latter." Rev. Samuel Rapaport, "The Midrash," in Rapaport, *Tales and Maxims from the Midrash* (N.p., 1907), 1, http://www.sacred-texts.com/jud/tmm/tmm02.htm.

[4] In the Koran, Abraham the smasher of idols is discussed in Chapter 19 (The Poets), and Abraham, Isaac, and the Aqedah are discussed in Chapter 37 (Those Who Rank Themselves in Order).

[5] Rev. Samuel Rapaport, "Genesis Rabba," in Rapaport, *Tales and Maxims from the Midrash,* 57, http://www.sacred-texts.com/jud/tmm/tmm07.htm.

[6] Genesis 18.

[7] The Azande of north-central Africa were famously studied by anthropologist Edward Evans-Pritchard in the 1930s. See E. E. Evans-Pritchard, *Witchcraft, Oracles and Magic among the Azande* (Oxford: Clarendon Press, 1937).

[8] Ernst Cassirer, *Mythical Thought,* vol. 2 of *The Philosophy of Symbolic Forms* (New Haven, Conn.: Yale University Press, 1955), p. xvi.

[9] This term is borrowed from Wolfgang Giegerich; see Giegerich, "The End of Meaning and the Birth of Man: An Essay about the State Reached in the History of Consciousness and an Analysis of C. G. Jung's Psychology Project," *Journal of Jungian Theory and Practice* 6, no. 1 (2004): 25.

[10] Ed Noort and Eibert Tigchelaar, *The Sacrifice of Isaac: The Aqedah (Genesis 22) and Its Interpretations* (Boston: Brill, 2002), pp. 1–21.

[11] "But no orphan will be he who, even in this tragic twentieth century, follows the father of some ancient and most modern men, Abraham from the land of Ur, the dualist and interactionist, who by indicating to us how to attune the earthly to the Imageless Transcendence, led us to hear 'Love thy God with all thy heart and all thy soul,' and 'Love thy neighbor as thyself.'" Silvano Arieti, *Abraham and the Contemporary Mind* (New York: Basic Books, 1981), pp. 179–180.

[12] See Shaoni Bhattacharya, "Elephants May Pay Homage to Dead Relatives," *New Scientist,* 26 October 2005.

[13] Space does not allow for a discussion of the formal contradictions between Jung's claim and the account of the Pueblo tribesman. See C. G. Jung, *The Symbolic Life: Miscellaneous Writings,* vol. 18 of *The Collected Works of C. G. Jung,* ed. and trans. Gerhard Adler and R. F. C. Hull (Princeton, N.J.: Princeton University Press, 1976), p. 274.

Innocence: Benign or Malignant?
Part 1: Clinical Struggles with Trauma in Light of Saint-Exupéry's *The Little Prince*

Donald E. Kalsched

Innocence is the crucial element in a person's spiritual nature.
—James S. Grotstein[1]

Real suffering belongs to innocence, not guilt.
—Helen Luke[2]

INTRODUCTION

My reflections on the subject of our conference, trust and betrayal, focus on that elusive essence at the very core of our sense of aliveness—something we call innocence that we associate with the guileless simplicity and wide-eyed trust of young children or the equally compelling beauty and presence of those special animals in our lives that we call pets. *Innocence* implies a virginal state connoting something pure, original, and uncontaminated by the "grown-up" or civilized world of adult experience. In Antoine de Saint-Exupéry's story *The Little Prince* we have a good example of such innocence, a child living alone on his tiny planet, soon to make a painful journey through the forest of experience to "this world."[3]

My interest in this topic of innocence comes mostly from my clinical work with a number of individuals, all of whom would be described, in the widely accepted terminology of Dr. Elaine Aron, as highly sensitive persons.[4] Because of their sensitive and highly attuned natures, these patients suffered significant relational trauma in their emotionally insensitive families—trauma severe enough in some cases to force them to withdraw parts of themselves into sanctuaries in the inner world for safekeeping.

The nature of these inner sanctuaries began to intrigue me because of what they contained and how they were defended. They usually contained a dependent, vulnerable, seemingly innocent part of the very young self (what Ronald Fairbairn and Harry Guntrip called the libidinal ego[5]) that is protected (and, at times, persecuted) by an aggressive system of inner objects that are ostensibly organized to protect the innocent child-part from further suffering. These sanctuaries are created *to keep something inviolate in the personality from being re-traumatized*; in other words, to keep it dissociated. Rapunzel shut in her tower by the witch is a good example from *Grimm's Fairy Tales*. I called this defensive system, with its innocent child-prisoner and its spell-casting guardian, the self-care system.[6]

Since the publication of my book *The Inner World of Trauma,* I have become better acquainted with the fields of affective neuroscience and attachment theory and have come to view the enclaves or sanctuaries in these persons' inner worlds as the result of very early, catastrophic injuries in the attachment relationship between infant and mother.[7] Relational trauma is the result, and it can be just as severe as the acute forms of abuse that result in dissociation and schizoid psychopathology. When the infant's generative innocence is unmet, unmediated into experience, it disappears from "this world" and takes up residence in "another world." This "other world" was known to Jung as the collective unconscious, the world of his number-two personality, or simply as "God's World." In this world, some innocent, pre-traumatic core of the infant has its life preserved "on another planet," but it is unable to *actualize* its core of aliveness until it comes into "this world."

In Saint-Exupéry's story, the little prince on his little planet up there in the sky is unable to really live and also, strangely, unable to die. These things can only happen "down here" in this world. Clinically, healing the split between these two worlds will mean a transformation in the self-care system so that the innocent part of the patient can be allowed to suffer experience again. One way this works is that the self-care system gets released into or outwardly enacted within the transference/countertransference relationship—and so does the child it contains. This can make for some very stormy and painful experience for both partners in the psychoanalytic adventure, as I will describe in a case below.

Two Worlds and Innocence as a Bridge between Them

Because childhood innocence is close to our original God-given nature—to our true, spontaneous selfhood—it tends to connote something of our divine inheritance, or what we think of as the human soul or spirit. There is something numinous about innocence. "Innocence is the crucial element in a person's spiritual nature," says Grotstein in the first epigraph for this chapter. That would put innocence very close to the human soul . . . *very close to an essential core of aliveness inside us and to the numinous mystery of that aliveness.*

Innocence is an ideal state, an archetypal ideal. In order to become fully human the innocent child in us will have to suffer through a trust and betrayal cycle on his or her way to becoming real. The romantic poet John Keats alluded to this necessary suffering in a letter he wrote to his brother George in 1819, in which he described what happens to innocence as it enters "this world":

> Call the world if you Please "The vale of Soul-making." Then
> you will find out the use of the world . . . . I say "*Soul-making*"—
> Soul as distinguished from an intelligence. There may be
> intelligence or sparks of the divinity in millions—but they are
> not Souls till they acquire identities, till each one is personally
> itself. Intelligences are atoms of perception—they know and they
> see and they are pure, in short they are God—how then are
> Souls to be made? How then are these sparks which are God to
> have identity given to them—so as ever to possess a bliss peculiar
> to each ones individual existence? How, but by the medium of
> a world like this? . . . Do you not see how necessary a World of
> Pains and troubles is to school an Intelligence and make it a soul?
> A Place where the heart must feel and suffer in a thousand diverse
> ways! . . . As various as the Lives of Men are—so various become
> their souls, and thus does God make individual beings, Souls,
> of the sparks of his own essence. This appears to me a faint
> sketch of a system of Salvation which does not affront our reason
> and humanity.[8]

Child Development: The Optimal Transition to Reality
So in Keats's view, the innocent soul, a divine substance or spark, is shaped by suffering as it confronts the pains and troubles of "this world." If we put this in the psychoanalytic language of child development, we would say that in the normal process of this descent, the innocent soul, reaching out for experience, is met by a reasonably empathic environment and the

soul takes up residence in the body. D. W. Winnicott called it the indwelling of the psyche in the soma,[9] and Heinz Kohut has helped us understand that the process involves a slow, incremental disillusionment, the result of which is the birth of internal psychic structure and a secure sense of self.[10] Attachment theory tells us that the psychosomatic attunement between infant and mother provides an intersubjective matrix for the soul's descent and that the result is secure attachment and an integrated ego. And contemporary neuroscience now informs us that without adequate attunement in the early infant/mother attachment bond, there are actual deficits in infant brain structure—especially in the right hemisphere and in the corpus callosum, the major link between left and right hemispheres. So a mediated descent into embodiment through the mother's empathy and attunement is critical for healthy development.

Developmentally then, we all start off as a human-divine unity, a wholeness, but the process of growing up, of developing a separate self, also means a "growing down,"[11] the descent of something daimonic or archetypal into limitation. It represents a fall away from that primordial sense of oneness in the Garden into twoness. In developing a self we inevitably become "self-centered" and self-conscious. We leave the garden of our innocence and now, knowing good and evil, live in exile—east of Eden, conscious but alienated.

Such alienation from our essential nature seems to be the necessary and inevitable price we pay for becoming conscious, and yet there remains within us a part of the original oneness that longs to return to that great spiritual reality from which we came and about which we have forgotten. This splinter of the divine radiance we call the soul, and its longing, Jung felt, was more than just a wish to return to the womb. He called this longing the religious instinct, which he held to be just as much a part of our instinctual equipment as the sexual instinct or the aggressive instinct or the instinct toward object-seeking. In fact, Jung said that we belong essentially to the species *Homo religiosus.* We are born from Spirit as well as from flesh. This gives us a dual destiny like the one suffered by Christ. But almost inevitably, we forget our spiritual home in God and become captivated by "this world."

When Transition between the Worlds Is Not Mediated: Impossible Suffering
So far, I've been exploring the optimal process of the soul's descent from "God's world." What about the situation where this process is less than optimal? What happens when the innocent child reaches out into this world and meets with pain it cannot negotiate? The short answer to that question

is that the child is traumatized. Trust is betrayed so badly that the reality of the world cannot be taken in.

Winnicott has reminded us that outer reality is a problem for all of us. If we are to become real and accept the otherness of reality, we first need an intermediate space in which our omnipotence and grandiosity (God's world) can mix and mingle with mundane reality. This is the space of paradox where things and people are both-and, not either/or—both inner and outer, self and other, divine and human. This paradoxical intermediate space invites the child into being. As Winnicott says, transitional space allows the child to stage its spontaneous gesture within "the area of omnipotence."[12] Gradually then, omnipotence can be given up and reality accepted. Omnipotence is slowly sloughed off or emptied out. The child can both find the world out there—separate—and simultaneously create it from "in here." So the world is both created and discovered. Trauma, says Grotstein, is when the infant encounters the real world too soon, before he or she has had a chance to create it.[13]

Trauma is universal in human life. We are always given experience that we are simply not equipped to experience. The mediating environment with its transitional aliveness breaks down. The world loses its function as a "vale of Soul-making" and the soul cannot enter, or if it has entered, it must leave.

Imagine a very small child—say an innocent little girl of three—reaching out in love toward a parental figure—say her father. Imagine that this happens when the alcoholic father is drunk and that he exploits his little girl's affection by violating her body, further terrifying her with threats if she tells. At traumatic moments such as this, the child faces the potential annihilation of her very personhood, the destruction of her personal spirit—soul murder, as Leonard Shengold called it.[14] This catastrophic possibility must be avoided at all costs, and so something quite extraordinary occurs. We tend to take this extraordinary thing for granted.

Suddenly she is on the ceiling, looking down at what is happening to her body, which she has vacated. If you are in an unbearable situation and you are helpless to leave, a part of you leaves, and for this to happen the whole self must split in two in order to prevent the unthinkable anxiety from being fully experienced. In this way dissociation divides us in two, but one part is preserved in what we call the unconscious—suspended there in its pristine condition while the other part grows up too fast and soldiers on in life, below, so to speak. We have reason to think that the nature of this splitting is universal. Part of the little girl in my example regresses back to an embryonic stage of relative innocence and safety prior to the trauma.

This regressed part will be buried deep in the body (the somatic unconscious) and will be protected by amnesia barriers thrown up by the defensive system. On the other hand, a separate part of the little girl progresses, grows up very fast, identifying with the aggressor and with the adult mind, transcending the immediate unbearable pain with a precocious philosophical, rational, and sometimes transcendent understanding. The progressed part then oversees the regressed part. In its protective role, it provides soothing like a guardian angel. At other times, in order to keep the regressed part inside, the progressed self may turn negative and become violent, imprisoning the regressed part and treating it sadistically. Its protection turns persecutory. In rare cases, if the outer trauma continues unabated and the person's essential core is in danger of annihilation, it becomes the task of the protector/persecutor to organize the child's suicide.[15]

So the inner division engineered by the self-care system preserves our innocence in some way, keeping this pre-trauma child-part with its divine spark out of suffering, assuring that it is never violated. This is its primary purpose. The innocence protected by the self-care system appears as a child in our dreams or (in the dreams of humankind that we call myths) as a child with royal or divine origins, like the little prince in our story. This child—male or female—represents a sacred core of personality and is referred to by different writers in different ways. Winnicott called it a "sacred incommunicado center" of the personality.[16] Guntrip referred to it as the "lost heart of the personal self."[17] Spiritually oriented psychotherapist A. H. Almaas says it's an ontological presence described simply as essence.[18] In *The Inner World of Trauma*, I refer to it as the "imperishable personal spirit" or "soul."[19] In our story, this essence is represented by the little prince on his planet.

MALIGNANT INNOCENCE: THE OMNIPOTENT, ENTITLED CHILD

However, preserving innocence on another planet in the psyche has a shadow side. What's not apparent in the little prince story, with its endearing innocence and its charming extra-planetary life, is *the violence that put him there in the first place and that threatens him every day of his existence.* I am referring to what Saint-Exupéry calls the "catastrophe of the baobabs."[20] As we read through the story we come to understand that the dreaded baobabs are a scourge on the little prince's planet. The "soil of the planet is infested" with their terrible seeds,[21] and they represent a continual threat, constantly springing up in a most demoralizing way, requiring constant vigilance and constant weeding. They threaten to turn the little prince's lovely planet into a nightmare of devastation. And it turns out, this threat of destruction is why the little prince has come to Earth in the first place, looking for a sheep to eat the baobabs and keep them from consuming everything good on his planet.

So along with innocence, there's an insidious and destructive force unfolding on the little prince's planet. How do we understand this? I've already noted that often when we find in the psyche of our traumatized patients a sanctuary of innocence, we also find very negative aggressive voices or powers that keep the "lost heart of the self" demoralized and hopeless about ever leaving the inner sanctum. Fairbairn has helped us here by demonstrating that in its defensive dynamics, the psyche uses its aggression for the purpose of self-splitting. He says that the child in a traumatogenic situation "uses a maximum of its aggression to subdue a maximum of its libidinal need."

> The splitting of the ego observed in the schizoid position is due to the operation of a certain volume of aggression which remains at the disposal of the central ego. It is this aggression that provides the dynamic of the severance of the subsidiary egos from the central ego. . . . The dynamic of repression is aggression.[22]

The aggression that Fairbairn is referring to here is not the normal healthy aggression that a child inevitably feels as it meets the frustrations of reality. Fairbairn is talking about inverted aggression, aggression now rebounding against the self. The child being abused identifies with the aggressor and joins him in an attack on the vulnerable core.

In Saint-Exupéry's story, the innocent child-part—now cut off from the world—starts to feel bad about himself. The terrible seeds of the baobab have infected his world and the voices of the attacking aggression now begin a litany of criticisms of the little prince. They accuse him of containing a bad seed, telling him that the seeds of the baobab growing inside are the real reason he is so alone and so cut off from the rest of humanity. His capacity for loving—in the story, his love for a single, unique, vulnerable rose—begins to be threatened.

Malignant Innocence: The Case of Helen
Consider the following situation: A little girl named Helen, aged four (later my patient), was brimming with excitement and hope as the family prepared to move into their first real home, where she had been promised her own room and a real backyard with a sandbox and a swing set.[23] The family

was gathered outside on this beautiful spring day, greeting the neighbors and getting acquainted as the moving van unloaded its cargo. In a creative act of inspiration, little Helen picked a handful of pretty yellow daffodils and enthusiastically handed them to her mother to celebrate this moment.

Here is an innocent act of love, done with great enthusiasm. The root of the word enthusiasm is *en-theos*—God or Spirit filling the person. We might say that something in little Helen's unique, God-given personal spirit was reaching across a threshold in a desire to come alive in the shared space with the mother in order to become real. This did not happen.

The mother looked down at the flowers and then quickly at the neighbor's yard and anxiously scolded her daughter, "No, no, Helen! What's the matter with you! How could you! You picked those flowers from Mrs. Smith's garden. Now you go and apologize to her!" Dragging the little girl by the arm, she forced an apology out of her and simultaneously broke her heart, destroying the hope implicit in this creative act, foreclosing the transitional space in which Helen's innocent aliveness was trying to connect to this world, to become real.

Now this is a perfectly common, ordinary moment in the lives of many children—a normal wounding that might or might not constitute a trauma, depending on the emotional resources available. But with my patient Helen, this kind of shaming by the narcissistic mother happened repeatedly. And there was no repair. Sixty years later, Helen remembered in her therapy the experience of inner disconnection on these occasions, of feeling nothing, feeling numb, distant, watching herself from another place in the room. Eventually she became good at this and even sought out the strange peace and quiet of the dissociated state.

Slowly Helen's growing disconnection from the mother became a disconnection from herself and from her body. The enthusiastic innocent child, reaching out, disappeared from Helen's outer life and took up residence in a separate world—in terms of our story, on another planet. From here it could emerge only in certain safe places in her life, in her private play with her dolls or with her beloved kitty cat or in her appreciation of nature or later in her reading of poetry. But strangely, these life-saving activities were increasingly surrounded by shame and guilt.

As her outer life hardened still further and Helen's energies were drawn increasingly into a busy, ambitious professional life, the soulful times when her little-girl-self could play became more and more rare, more and more remote, more and more forgotten. She became angry and cynical and bitter. Now her grown-up self began to hate her inner child because of its neediness and its dependency, and she began to hate the imperfect, inferior "fat" body where it lived. She was constantly on guard against humiliation and was filled with judgment and shame. The mother's voice was now her inner voice of self-denial. Whenever her innocent child-self reached out into the world, she heard "No, no, Helen, what's the matter with you!" Soon she refused to participate with the family in activities. She ran away from home. She picked fights with other kids at school. It wasn't long before she developed an eating disorder and started wishing that she were a boy. She became depressed and her suffering increased. By the time I met her fifty years later she was a very successful corporate lawyer, but inwardly she was in despair.

Before Helen finally surrendered to therapy, she had tried to turn her inner suffering into a meaningful life by pursuing outer causes. She became an animal rights activist and spent a lot of time rescuing innocent animals that had been run over on the roads near her house. She became a child-care worker and an anti-abortion activist who would sometimes talk appreciatively of the men who shot down abortion doctors in order to protect unborn innocent children. (This was very unnerving to me.) Psychologically, identification with innocent victims is often a substitute for grief and mourning, and Helen repeatedly took this bypass.

In short, Helen's original childhood innocence had become malignant. It was fueling her rage and her wish for revenge. She no longer had access to her true innocence inwardly but projected it everywhere—onto animals and unborn babies and people who had been persecuted, whom she defended. She saw the entire world in terms of innocent victims and evil persecutors, but she could not see the innocence in herself or the evil perpetrators. She was living in a projected world, in which both sides of the self-care system were only "out there" in the world.

Working with Malignant Innocence: Stories and Interpretations
We all tell ourselves stories in order to make meaning of our lives. Many of these stories are unconscious to those of us afflicted with trauma's legacy. With such persons the story usually includes simultaneously a deep love of innocent life, on the one hand, and a deep unconscious conviction of badness and a fear of discovery, on the other. When the innocence is projected, trauma survivors often become great healers of others, great reformers with a genuine passion for innocent victims. But they rarely encounter their own innocent suffering or get to their own reformations, their own transformations.

In a similar way, when the sense of badness is projected, the trauma survivor finds himself in a menacing world full of potential perpetrators.

The world is a frightening place, and the goodness of one's rose is under constant threat, as in *The Little Prince*. Baobabs threaten from inside, but the person doesn't know this. Instead there is a perceived threat of rejection or humiliation from the environment. Such a person is always on guard against the evil intentions in others, always afraid of being humiliated or shamed and always convinced that the last time they spoke up, or loved a rose, they put themselves in danger, or humiliated themselves.

So the inner story of the trauma survivor provides an interpretation that contains suffering, causes suffering, and mobilizes action—action designed to prevent suffering in the innocent both "out there" and "in here." The suffering of their repetitive stories is chronic and built around a great sense of outrage, a sense of personal violation, of refusal to admit to the inferiority one feels. Indeed, one could say that the whole self-care story, with all its suffering, is designed to avoid a more acute form of suffering, the suffering contained in the innocent core of oneself, now burdened with some terrible darkness and shame.

So in therapy, or in life, what would surrendering this defense look like? Well, it would mean surrendering the story that projects innocence and evil "out there." It would mean compassion for the generative innocence *in oneself* and sympathy for how terribly injured it has been— by life first and then by one's own self-protection. It would mean simply feeling that hurt, letting it out, crying its tears, without an explanation and without blame.

This is apparently impossible to do without love. The transformative tears of this unguarded hurt apparently have to be shed with another who understands. This kind of love invites the sequestered innocent child back into existence. We will see, in Part 2, how the little prince in our story brings his innocence down to Earth and teaches the pilot how to love, lessons he's learned from the fox.

A big part of therapy is encouraging an individual to reflect on the ways this inner victim/perpetrator story is unfolding its tragic drama in his or her life, usually alienating everyone. This is what I had to do with Helen. When we interpret in psychoanalysis, often what we're doing is offering an alternative interpretation to the interpretation—the story—that is whispered daily by the self-care system into the ears of our traumatized patients. I had to help Helen understand that her interpretation of experience in terms of the victim/persecutor scenario was her way of staying unconscious of that innocent part of herself that carried the spark of her God-given true self. I had to convince her to let this "lost heart of herself" come into relationship with me, and this meant opening my heart to the possibility of loving her also. Analytic training does not prepare us for this or for the necessary suffering involved in sacrificing this love to the work of analysis.

BEYOND INTERPRETATION

So far I've been discussing the classical way we have always worked in psychoanalysis, through interpretation and the quest for meaning. Beyond interpretation there are other ways of working with people in whom innocence has become an "extraterrestrial." In these more relational methods, we have to enter the story and become one of its actors. We have to let innocence come down to Earth right there in our consulting rooms and learn to relate to it. As the fox taught the little prince (as we shall see in Part 2), this means letting ourselves be tamed . . . letting ourselves care about the patient and the work, more than we "should." And it is apparently not enough to just love the little prince (in our patients) into earthly existence. There are also the baobabs and the snake in the story of the little prince, and they are continually attacking love and filling it with grief—the grief of loss, the grief of disappointment, the grief of disillusionment with ourselves and our innocent expectations of therapy and what it can do.

So with Helen, I had to live through a process of having my own innocence and good intentions transformed by her incessant attacks. I was always failing Helen in some way, and this made me feel bad. I once forgot her appointment and found her in the waiting room with another client. I almost always failed to give her enough notice about my vacations or necessary breaks in the schedule. I was avoiding injuring her innocence and provoking its frightening rageful guardian. I didn't want her to withdraw to her planet again. I didn't want to have to come and get her again. I didn't want the *Sturm und Drang* of dragging her innocent child into experience . . . necessary experience. I would rather have colluded with her and protected her innocence . . . and mine.

In order to make this experience possible, I had to receive her rage and anger at these times and admit to my own failings. I had to take on some of the badness consciously without defending my own version of innocence. When she saw my genuine human struggle, my real sorrow and irritation with her, my disappointment in myself, my defensive excuses finally acknowledged, she could allow the "little princess" in herself to attach once again. At the same time she was released somewhat from her own shame and I became that object in the transference that she could destroy, then say hello to . . . and then love again. For me this meant a certain voluntary surrender of innocence.

Over the last twenty years, clinicians working with early-trauma patients have made a painful discovery; namely, that the usual analytic situation, with its emphasis on words, its power differential between patient and analyst, and its tendency to objectify the patient through interpretation, often re-traumatizes the very people it was designed to help. It became clear that work with trauma survivors requires much greater mutuality, transparency, and affect-attunement in the analytic partnership, reminiscent of the early mother-child interaction.

Analysts have begun to realize that *what has been broken relationally must be repaired relationally*. The early attachment problem that occurred with the mother reenters the relationship with the therapist, where a real repair is possible. But if this is to occur, the therapist must constantly monitor his or her injured innocence and the impulse to withdraw from the patient. We all know those moments. We start to think the patient needs medication. Or we hear ourselves making a sadistically tinged interpretation. Or we start to think of referring the patient. This is what the repetition compulsion looks like. As against this tendency to withdraw, we must tune in on an affect level to those dissociative gaps or places of derailment where the intimate feeling-connection with the patient is threatening to come apart. The work of Philip Bromberg provides many examples of this delicate negotiation and how the analyst must become a full partner in the dyadic regulation of affect and the co-creation of an entirely new intersubjective reality.[24] Fortunately, in this process, what the analyst says or does will be less important than "how openly what does happen is processed with the analysand."[25]

We come back, then, to the idea of two worlds that we started with. In Helen's situation, the divine world with its "extraterrestrial" energies, including the innocent soul-carrying child, had been co-opted in the service of defense against the realities of living. This left a picture just like the one Freud described: inflation, malignant innocence, negative grandiosity, infantile omnipotence, neurotic suffering, all organized by a self-care system in order to avoid the impossible suffering of life in reality. But the numinous aura around this core of innocence was not produced by the repression. *The divine child within us is not an artifact of the defensive process but the very thing the defensive process is protecting. And it is protecting it because it is divine—the very core of our aliveness.*

For my patient Helen, and for all of us, the normal stress of therapy requires that the divine (archetypal) world be freed from its recruitment as a defense in order to perform its proper function of enlightening her/our earthbound suffering with its redeeming presence. In the process, our neurotic suffering slowly gets changed—not to everyday misery, as Freud suggested, but into what Wordsworth called the "still, sad music of humanity."[26] We take on a piece of the darkness of the world and carry it. This leads to en*light*enment. Suddenly there is meaning, joy, and gratitude. A little prince comes into the desert of our lives and says, "Draw me a sheep."

NOTES

[1] James S. Grotstein, "Forgery of the Soul," in *Evil: Self & Culture,* ed. Mary Coleman Nelson and Michael Eigen (New York: Human Sciences Press, 1984), p. 213.

[2] Helen Luke, *The Way of Woman: Awakening the Perennial Feminine* (New York: Doubleday, 1995), p. 60.

[3] Antoine de Saint-Exupéry, *The Little Prince,* trans. Irene Testot-Ferry (Hertfordshire, England: Wordsworth Classics, 1995).

[4] Elaine Aron, *The Highly Sensitive Person: How to Thrive When the World Overwhelms You* (New York: Broadway Books, 1996).

[5] See W. Ronald D. Fairbairn, *Psychoanalytic Studies of the Personality* (1952; London: Routledge and Kegan Paul, 1981); and Harry Guntrip, *Psychoanalytic Theory, Therapy, and the Self: A Basic Guide to the Human Personality in Freud, Erickson, Klein, Sullivan, Fairbairn, Hartmann, Jacobson, and Winnicott* (New York: Basic Books, 1969).

[6] Donald Kalsched, *The Inner World of Trauma: Archetypal Defenses of the Personal Spirit* (London: Routledge, 1996).

[7] *Ibid.*

[8] John Keats to George and Georgiana Keats, [28 April] 1819, in *Letters of John Keats to His Family and Friends,* ed. Sidney Colvin (London: McMillan and Company, 1891), pp. 255–256. Keats's italics.

[9] Donald Woods Winnicott, "On the Basis for Self in Body" (1970), in *Psychoanalytic Explorations,* ed. Claire Winnicott, Ray Shepherd, and Madeleine Davis (Cambridge, Mass.: Harvard University Press, 1989), p. 271.

[10] Heinz Kohut, *The Restoration of the Self* (New York: International Universities Press, 1977).

[11] See James Hillman, *The Soul's Code: In Search of Character and Calling* (New York: Random House, 1996), pp. 41–62.

[12] Donald Woods Winnicott, "The Concept of Trauma in Relation to the Development of the Individual within the Family" (1965), in *Psychoanalytic Explorations,* ed. Claire Winnicott, Ray Shepherd, and Madeleine Davis (Cambridge, Mass.: Harvard University Press, 1989), p. 145.

[13] James S. Grotstein, *Who Is the Dreamer Who Dreams the Dream? A Study of Psychic Presences* (London: Analytic Press, 2000).

[14] Leonard Shengold, *Soul Murder: The Effects of Childhood Abuse and Deprivation* (New York: Fawcett Columbine, 1989).

[15] Sandor Ferenczi, *The Clinical Diary of Sandor Ferenczi,* ed. Judith Dupont, trans. Michael Balint and Nicola Z. Jackson (Cambridge, Mass.: Harvard University Press, 1988), p. 10.

[16] D. W. Winnicott, "Communicating and Not Communicating Leading to a Study of Certain Opposites" (1963), in Winnicott, *The Maturational Processes and the Facilitating Environment: Studies in the Theory of Emotional Development* (London: Hogarth Press, 1965), p. 187.

[17] Guntrip, *Psychoanalytic Theory,* p. 172.

[18] A. H. Almaas, *Essence: The Diamond Approach to Inner Realization* (York Beach, Maine: Samuel Weiser, Inc., 1998), pp. 76–82.

[19] Kalsched, *The Inner World of Trauma.*

[20] Saint-Exupéry, *The Little Prince,* p. 24.

[21] *Ibid.,* p. 26.

[22] Fairbairn, *Psychoanalytic Studies of the Personality,* p. 108.

[23] In order to preserve confidentiality, I have fictionalized certain details of this case study by creating an amalgam of material from more than one patient.

[24] Philip Bromberg, *Awakening the Dreamer: Clinical Journeys* (Mahwah, N.J.: Analytic Press, 2006).

[25] Stephen A. Mitchell, *Relational Concepts in Psychoanalysis: An Integration* (Cambridge, Mass.: Harvard University Press, 1988), p. x.

[26] William Wordsworth, "Lines Composed a Few Miles above Tintern Abbey" (1798), in *The Collected Poems of William Wordsworth,* intro. Antonia Till (Hertfordshire, England: Wordsworth Editions Limited, 2006), p. 243.

4, Part 2

Innocence: Benign or Malignant?
Part 2: The Child between the Worlds

Donald E. Kalsched

> *On the seashore of endless worlds, children meet.*
> —Rabindranath Tagore[1]

This epigraph from Tagore (which was one of Winnicott's favorites) expresses the "between" space of "the child between the worlds" and also hides a spiritual reality . . . "endless worlds." As we've seen, this paradoxical or transitional space—between the worlds—is where the little prince travels in his journey back and forth.

THE LITTLE PRINCE

Here is an abridged version of the story with psychological commentary. An innocent little prince lives on his tiny perfumed planet (asteroid B-612), tenderly watering his beloved single rose, devotedly cleaning his three tiny volcanoes, and diligently moving his chair forty-four times so he can enjoy the beauty of multiple sunsets. Listening every night to the music in the stars up there, he lives contentedly in his own world. As yet, he doesn't know he's lonely. He has not yet risked betrayal in order for his innocence to be transformed by experience.

Then there are the so-called grown-ups. They occupy a parallel universe in the story (some of them live on asteroids too), and they all seem to be embodiments of emptiness and absurdity. There is a pilot, too, who is very grown up, but his life has come to a dead end. He's crashed his plane in the Sahara Desert and is trying to repair his engine. The story tells us that as a child the pilot had a vivid imagination just like the little prince, but he has forgotten. As a child, he would produce drawings of boa constrictors digesting elephants, but because his first drawings showed only the outside of the boa constrictors, the grown-ups around him all thought they were hats! So he drew more pictures of boa constrictors, showing the inside with the elephant being digested. But the grownups never understood his drawings and slowly, sadly, he gave up drawing boa constrictors from the outside and the inside. Instead, he spoke only of golf, bridge, politics, and neckties. Thereafter the grownups found him to be a very sensible person. But something in him was no longer alive, except maybe when he flew his airplane.

So the two worlds in our story—the magical world of childhood, on the one hand, innocent and full of mystery and imagination, and the grown-up world, on the other hand, full of sensible things, albeit meaningless empty and boring—these two worlds that we might think of as the fertile unconscious, on the one hand, and the dried-up, one-sided ego, on the other—are separated by cosmic distances. Just like in the individuation process, a major dynamic of the story is the separation between these two worlds and how this will be resolved. Each is incomplete without the other. The little prince is quintessentially alive but is all alone on his own planet—and therefore unrealized—living in a bubble of unknowing naïveté. The pilot is going through the motions of life, having become a very sensible, worldly man, rushing around doing important things, but without a soul.

If life is to be lived to its fullest—if wholeness is to be realized—then these separate worlds will have to get together. This will require a particular kind of conscious suffering—a particular depth of suffering—that neither the little prince nor the crashed pilot has experienced before. The suffering required in this process has to do with enormous sadness and grief, consciously experienced. This grief seems to happen *only where the two worlds meet and are held in tension consciously.* Innocence must suffer experience and in this sense suffer betrayal and disillusionment. At the same time, the dried-up ego-dominated world of the pilot must suffer the grief of loss and re-illusionment, which means feeling things that have been repressed or forsaken and allowing life to be reanimated by contact with the other world of the little prince. In effect, this will constitute the return of the soul to the body . . . the return of aliveness and meaning.

As the little prince begins his journey to Earth—moving from one asteroid to another—his experience of betrayal begins. His first moment of disillusionment comes with a geographer, who tells him that his beloved rose is not even worth recording in his book because it is ephemeral and will die. The little prince suddenly is confronted by the reality of death, and he is flooded with a feeling of great vulnerability. He feels guilty that he left his rose so unprotected. He begins to feel very troubled by a new awareness. He starts to be lonely for companionship. He wishes he could find somebody to talk to.

He next comes to Earth and, true to our Western origin myth, meets the snake. He asks the snake why there are no men in the desert. The snake can see that the little prince is still mostly innocent, having just fallen from a star, and he feels sorry about what lies ahead on this Earth. He assures the little prince that if things get too bad for him, he can get him back to his home planet in no time . . . with just one little bite. The little prince understands perfectly. Here the snake, like Lucifer in the Genesis account, stands for consciousness, but also for unconsciousness through dissociation. When experience gets to be too much, he can put you in an altered state and remove you back home, just like the self-care system of traumatized people does.

Armed with this new knowledge, the little prince continues his journey in search of companions. On a lonely mountain peak he cries out, "Be my friends, I am all alone." An echo answers, "I am all alone . . . all alone . . ."[2] And then the real pain begins. The little prince stumbles into a garden of 5,000 roses and is overcome with another disillusionment. His single rose had told him that she was the only flower of her kind in all the world, but she had lied to him! She was just a common rose and that's all he had had all along, together with three motley volcanoes, one of which was extinct! Suddenly he didn't feel like a very great prince, and he lay on the grass and cried.

And at this crucial moment, the fox appears and the little prince finds his first friend on Earth. The fox is a kind of psychopomp who teaches the little prince how to love, and his lessons are movingly relevant to our work as therapists, so I want to follow the dialogue rather closely. "'Come and play with me,' suggested the little prince . . . 'I am so terribly sad . . . ' 'I cannot play with you,' said the fox. 'I am not tame.' 'Oh! I'm so sorry,' said the little prince. . . . 'But . . . what does "tame" mean?'"[3]

The fox then explains that tame means "to establish ties." (Perhaps the fox is an attachment theorist!) This confuses the little prince, so the fox explains further:

> To me, you are still just a little boy like a hundred thousand
> other little boys. And I have no need of you. And you have no
> need of me, either. To you, I am just a fox like a hundred
> thousand other foxes. But if you tame me, we shall need one

another. To me, you will be unique. And I shall be unique to
you. . . . My life will be full of sunshine. I shall recognize the
sound of a step different from all others. The other steps send
[me] hurrying underground. Yours will call me out of my burrow
like the sound of music. And look yonder. Do you see the [golden
wheat]fields? . . . You have hair [of the same] colour. . . . So it
will be marvelous when you have tamed me! The [golden] wheat
will remind me of you. And I shall love the sound of the wind
in the wheat.[4]

All right, all right, says the little prince, I'll tame you. But "what should
I do?" The fox replies, "You must be very patient. . . . First you will sit
down at a little distance from me, like that, in the grass. I shall watch you
out of the corner of my eye and you will say nothing. Words are a source
of misunderstandings. But every day, you can sit a little closer to me."[5]
And so it was that the little prince tamed the fox.

And there was something else the fox taught the little prince. Taming
doesn't work right unless the little prince comes back every day *at the
same time.* The fox informs him that he "must observe certain rites";
that is, he must come at regular times so that the meetings are honored
as special and can be anticipated.[6] And also, the fox tells him, if a new
friend doesn't show up at the appointed time, well then, you'll "discover
the price of happiness."[7]

This is a beautiful example of how the therapy hour and the analytic
frame actualizes a different kind of time, separating sacred time from
profane time, *kairos* from *chronos.* This regularity, says the fox, is an
important part of proper taming.

Finally the little prince must take his leave and the fox says, "Oh!
. . . I shall cry."

> "It is your own fault," said the little prince. "I wished you
> no harm but you wanted me to tame you."
> "Yes, indeed," said the fox.
> "But you are going to cry!" said the little prince.
> "That is so," said the fox.
> "Then it has not helped you in any way!"
> "It *has* helped me," said the fox, "because of the colour
> of the wheatfields."[8]

We could spend our whole time together on that statement and its
implications for the necessary suffering-into-reality that is part of
individuation. It suggests that the apprehension of beauty and the act of

loving go hand in hand and somehow make loss—even the loss of life itself—worth it, "because of the wheatfields."

As therapists we also must heed the lessons of the fox about taming and wheatfields. We must find a way to reach the shy and mute children inside our traumatically wounded patients just like the little prince tamed the fox. We must make a safe space. We must open our hearts to the invisible realities of the human soul and learn the value of silence and poetry and embodied presence, without interpretation. There is no rational diagnostic understanding of a patient without first taming them. This is the lesson of the fox.

This is also the lesson of contemporary neuroscience as applied to psychotherapy with trauma survivors. We will never reach the split-off innocent core of our patients, says Allan N. Schore, unless we learn to attune to the "implicit relational knowing" of right-brain to right-brain communication.[9] Preverbal relational trauma is encoded in the right hemisphere. We must therefore bypass the word-strewn left hemisphere with its higher rational understandings and interpretations if we are ever to reach the planet where the injured, innocent child lives—in our patients and in ourselves.

To return to the story, the little prince has been on Earth for almost a year when he finally runs into a human being—the stranded airplane pilot. The pilot is asleep on the sand and the little prince wakes him with a request: "Please . . . draw me a sheep."[10]

The pilot is completely thunderstruck. He rubs his eyes, blinks hard, and looks carefully around. He sees an extraordinary little boy watching him gravely. The pilot then draws him the only thing he knows how to draw—a boa constrictor from the outside with an elephant inside that looks to all the grownups like a hat. The pilot is astonished when the little fellow says, "No! No! I don't want an elephant inside a boa. A boa constrictor is very dangerous creature and an elephant is very cumbersome. Everything is very small where I live. I need a sheep. Draw me a sheep."[11] So the pilot, now suddenly awakened to his earlier forgotten artistic life, draws a sheep.

In this charming initial contact, we have a wonderful example of a connection made on the level of the child. Child to child, one might say. The pilot has not met anyone in thirty years who understood his drawing, and the little prince has not met a grownup who understood, as the fox said, that "it is only with one's heart that one can see clearly."[12]

I think there are moments like this in the psychotherapy situation where true healing begins. The most obvious would be moments where the patient feels deeply understood for perhaps the first time in a long time. But such moments happen for the therapist as well. Perhaps the genuine innocent yearning in the child inside the patient awakens in the therapist his or her own longings and a heartfelt smile is exchanged between the analytic partners that says everything. Often the child-to-child moments are completely unplanned. A funny moment in which the therapist says something totally absurd or puts his foot in it somehow . . . or a story the patient tells that tickles the funny bone of the therapist so that mutual laughter breaks out, dissolving both partners in laughter that won't stop.

In the next stage of our story, we find the little prince teaching the pilot the lessons he's learned from the fox. It has now been eight days since the pilot has broken down, and he is out of water. The little prince suggests they go look for a well in the desert—a very stupid idea, the pilot thinks. But somehow he has been touched by the little prince, so he consents. They walk all day and into the night, finally sitting down under the stars in silent reverie. The little prince says, "The stars are beautiful . . . because of a flower you cannot see." He continues, "What makes the desert so beautiful . . . is that it hides a well, somewhere . . ."[13]

The pilot begins to understand that the invisible secrets hidden in the human heart are the source of life's beauty and meaning, and suddenly he is deeply moved. He picks up the sleeping little prince in his arms and walks into the night. He is suddenly in touch with the exquisite beauty and vulnerability of that fragile innocent creature in his arms:

> It seemed to me I was carrying a very fragile treasure. It even seemed to me that there was nothing more fragile on all the Earth. In the moonlight I gazed at the pale forehead, the closed eyes, the locks of hair trembling in the breeze, and said to myself: "What I see here is nothing but a shell. What is important is invisible. . . . "
>
> As his lips opened slightly with the suspicion of a half-smile, I said to myself once again: "What moves me so deeply about this little prince sleeping here is his loyalty to a flower. The image of a rose shining through his whole being like the flame of a lamp even when he is asleep. . . ." And I felt him to be more fragile still. Lamps should be protected with great care: a gust of wind can extinguish them. . . .
>
> And I walked on and at daybreak I discovered the well.[14]

And the well they discover is no ordinary well. It is a magical well with a bucket and a pulley that sings as the bucket is lowered. Like the biblical story of Jesus at the well, it contains living water, the water of life. "This water was something entirely different from ordinary nourishment," realized the pilot. "It was born from the walk under the stars, the singing of the pulley and the effort of my arms. It was good for the heart, like a gift."[15]

Suddenly the pilot feels overwhelmed with grief. He begins to realize that the little prince is planning to leave him, to return to his star and his rose, and that he has made a pact with the snake to end his suffering on Earth and return to his planet. The pilot tries to prevent this, tries to kill the snake who will do this dirty deed, but the little prince has already made his decision. It is the anniversary of his coming to Earth, his star will be exactly above the spot where he came down, and now he must go home— home to his rose.

"Once again," says the pilot, "I was frozen by a sense of something irreparable. And I realized that I couldn't bear the thought of never hearing that laughter again. It was like a spring of fresh water in the desert for me."[16] The little prince can sense the pilot's fear, so, in a repeat of his parting from the fox, from whom he had learned about the wheatfields, he reassures the pilot that their inevitable parting will be assuaged by a gift. It will be the gift of his laughter.

"What are you saying?" asks the incredulous pilot. The little prince explains. It's the same explanation the fox gave him. It has to do with wheatfields.

> "When you look up at the sky at night, since I shall be living on one of them and laughing on one of them, for you it will be as if all the stars were laughing. You and only you will have stars that can laugh!" And as he said it he laughed.
>
> "And when you are comforted you will be happy to have known me. You will always be my friend. You will want to laugh with me. And from time to time you will open your window, just for the pleasure of it. . . . And your friends will be astonished to see you laughing whilst gazing at the sky. And so you will say to them, 'Yes, stars always make me laugh' and they will think you are crazy. I shall have played a very naughty trick on you. . . ." And once again he laughed. "It will be as if I had given you, instead of stars, a lot of little bells that can laugh."[17]

Six years later, as the pilot relates his story, he acknowledges that he has overcome a part of his great sorrow through the gift the little prince left him, but only a part. He realizes that his great sadness is the inevitable price for loving someone. As the fox said, "One runs the risk of crying a bit if one allows oneself to be tamed."[18] And he listens to the stars at night, like five hundred million little bells, and sometimes the little bells all change themselves into tears. But nothing in the universe can ever be the same, because the little prince has been here and a path between the worlds has been opened. Now there is the magic of wheatfields and the laughing stars with their special invisible secret that only he and his little friend share.

BARBARA

When our patients come into treatment, they often do not know that they house within themselves a little prince on another planet. They may have a vague sense of something inside that has been lost—something sacred, which is why they come to a Jungian analyst. But the path between the worlds has been blocked. Sometimes it takes months or years to make contact with this innocent part of the personality, like aboriginal Stone Age people in the Amazon jungle who weren't discovered by Western anthropologists until the 1960s or 70s. But then, sometimes through a dream or a shared moment of connection, contact will be made with the little prince part of the personality. Here is an example of this kind of surprising contact, with a patient I call Barbara.

Barbara had an important, mystical dream. I was not working with her at the time she had this dream. It occurred as she was settling into her first Jungian analysis in another city with a female colleague she had consulted for anxiety and depression. She had grown up as the over-responsible oldest daughter in an upper-middle-class family with a handsome, charismatic, but emotionally remote father whom she adored and an emotionally unstable, narcissistic mother whom she came to fear.

Her mother's irrational outbursts were truly terrifying to young Barbara. She remembered hardening herself on the outside, trying to "be good" and tiptoe around the mother's rages, all the while removing a part of herself emotionally on the inside, feeling angry, shameful, and bad. "I went to a cold, remote place," she said. Then her psyche sent her this dream from that cold remote place.

Green Monster Dream
> I'm on a cold, dying planet, like what the arctic might be without snow. I'm a scout for an animal preservation center. I am on this planet to pick up surviving creatures—this time, a baby mammal similar to a bear cub. It would die here and it's the last of its kind.
>
> I'm picking up the cub-creature from a way station. The cub was found and brought here by a being I know as the

emissary. The only hardy form of life in this eerie, gray world, this emissary searches out surviving creatures for transport to earth. The emissary remains behind a wall in the building because humans cannot tolerate his form. It is his choice to remain there, for the wall protects him from human revulsion. I find the emissary's mission and his plight very poignant.

I see the little cub, wrapped in a dirty, almost slimy fur blanket, rather like a polar bear's coat. I suddenly realize the blanket is alive—it's another creature from this planet. The voice of the emissary behind the wall is telling me how to care for the cub, and he explains that he found the blanket animal out there too, also abandoned. It kept the cub warm, and he hopes we will take it back to earth also. The emissary's voice is clear, cultured, and kind. I wonder how a being with such a beautiful voice can be too ugly to be seen.

I suddenly realize that the emissary loves the blanket animal deeply. I, on the other hand, am repulsed by it, and the emissary knows it. The blanket animal wrapped around the cub smells, and its nature somehow seems slug-like. My clothes will be ruined from holding the blanket creature, but pity seizes me: it can't help what it is and deserves to live. My clothes don't matter, or my disgust either. We will take the blanket creature and the cub back to earth and do the best we can for them both. I am struck with the thought of differences and the need for acceptance.

I pick up both creatures and prepare to leave. Then the emissary asks if I would mind if he held the blanket creature (with its wrapped-up cub) just one more time. I am achingly moved. I suddenly wonder if it is a baby of his kind and if that is why he hides. The emissary tells me to step close to the wall, a smooth metallic surface in which there is a round opening. I step forward, and a bright green tentacle comes out and waves around searching for contact.

I'm frozen in horror. I don't withdraw, partly because I can't react fast enough and partly because I said he could touch. The tentacle shoots out, wrapping itself under my bundle and catching on my clothing—ugh! The tentacle corrects, wraps around all of us in a tight squeeze, and retracts. It was all so quick! Now I know why the emissary must remain behind the wall: he is a green monster.

Barbara and her first analyst worked on that dream for a long time. Ten years later, when she moved to New York and we began our work together, the dream was still alive for her, and so was the question about its mysterious meaning. "I suffered that monster and loved him fiercely," Barbara said to me, "but I could not get him to earth in a way that felt real. Somehow that's my job here with you."

Intuitively, I felt she was probably right but I had no idea what to think about the Green Monster or how we might help him come to Earth. Perhaps, I thought, her dream was giving her a chance to feel love and compassion for an innocent part of *herself* that was basically loving and good but so encumbered by shame that it had to be walled off. The monster's green tentacle reached out in love for one last contact with the blanket baby. This led me to wonder if perhaps he embodied Barbara's early instinct for attachment itself, an instinct that in its innocence had been badly injured and shamed and had now retired to its dying planet, never to reach out again . . . until now, in this dream, perhaps because of the safety of her newfound therapy.

And the monster is green! Green is the color of life in its vegetative form, so the monster would seem to be centrally concerned with life, especially endangered life. He searches it out and saves it for eventual transfer to Earth, where presumably it needs to go in order to come alive again. Combing his dying planet for endangered life forms, he serves as a kind of psychic container and mediator, a soul-holder for Barbara's animated core of aliveness that is marooned on another world until she is ready to receive it back into her worldly life.

Is this not a beautiful thing the psyche does? Holding our innocence and our aliveness for us until such time as this innocent aliveness is ready for experience? And then providing mediation from the inner world? It moves me just to think about it, and it moved Barbara too, especially as she felt the particular plight of the Green Monster, the deep loving attachment it had with the blanket-creature and its baby. For Barbara, the poignant thing about this love was the inevitable loss it entailed. As we've already witnessed, this combination of love and loss is the central agony in *The Little Prince*.

If we translate this into psychological language, we would say that the innocent life in us cannot continue unless it leaves its encapsulation—its planet—in the unconscious and enters the flow of life and suffering "here below." This means a great sorrow, a great grief. Like the pilot in our story, Barbara had met her little prince and discovered his lesson of love and his voluntary sacrifice. And part of this lesson—the part that's so hard to grasp for those of us who have not had our innocent selves lovingly mediated into being in this world—is that the two worlds must stay separated, *except for a symbolic link*—for example, wheatfields. The Green Monster cannot leave his planet. The little prince also must return to his world, forever separated, but the link between the worlds is life-giving— absolutely essential if the soul is to live in the world. And this possibility of aliveness wrapped in sorrow emerges when something more is glimpsed between the worlds if that intermediate space has been quickened by human love. The little prince in our story is an emissary of this love. He is a child negotiating between the worlds of innocence and experience, a divine child who carries both worlds in himself as his own tragic and beautiful dual destiny.

As Barbara and I began our analytic adventure together against the backdrop of her Green Monster dream, her psyche began to portray in dreams further evidence that something dreadful had happened to her and her innocence—some kind of early attachment trauma when she was very young. For ten years we have worked together on that story and made some fascinating discoveries together, and we have also relived the early attachment trauma in the transference and survived it together. In fact it could be said that we repaired something that we could gain access to only by reenacting and suffering it together.

CONCLUSION

The Little Prince holds important lessons. Among other things, it suggests that we cannot (apparently) become fully human until we can accept the human condition and that we cannot accept the human condition until we have accepted this difficult reality—*that we must let the innocent part of us suffer in order to grow a soul.* We have to let ourselves be tamed. And if we carry a history of severe early trauma, the risk of this is going to feel very great indeed. If we are lucky, this process of taming will take place slowly, through love (relationship) and the experience of beauty (art), so that the magic of transitional aliveness—foreclosed by trauma—can be rekindled once again.

Once we have the courage to engage this difficult process, we can get to the joy on the other side of it, the sheer ecstasy of being alive . . . wheatfields and star-music. The myth seems to say that if we consciously, voluntarily, and ritually allow innocence to suffer experience it will lead to the indwelling of the soul and communion with a great mystery at the center of life. We cannot ask for more than that.

NOTES

[1] Rabindranath Tagore, "On the Seashore," in Tagore, *The Crescent Moon: Child Poems* (New York: Macmillan, 1913), p. 3, also available at the website of the Poetry Foundation, www.poetryfoundation.org/archive/poem.html?id=174939.

[2] Saint-Exupéry, *The Little Prince,* p. 72.

[3] *Ibid.,* p. 76.

[4] *Ibid.,* p. 77.

[5] *Ibid.,* p. 79.

[6] *Ibid.,* p. 80.

[7] *Ibid.,* p. 79.

[8] *Ibid.,* p. 80. My italics.

[9] Allan N. Shore, *Affect Regulation and Repair of the Self* (New York: W. W. Norton, 2003).

[10] Saint-Exupéry, *The Little Prince,* p. 12.

[11] *Ibid.,* p. 14.

[12] *Ibid.,* p. 82.

[13] *Ibid.,* p. 89.

[14] *Ibid.,* p. 90.

[15] *Ibid.,* p. 93.

[16] *Ibid.,* p. 99.

[17] *Ibid.,* p. 100.

[18] *Ibid.,* p. 95.

5

Trust and Betrayal in Adult Relationships*

Deborah Egger-Biniores

I n the nineteenth century the term "odyssey" was adopted into everyday English usage as depicting a long and adventurous wandering. It is still used today in a similar manner, sometimes shortened to the concept of an epic voyage. There is no more adventurous voyage than the one that involves trust and betrayal in adult relationships.

As in Homer's *Odyssey,* we have a strikingly modern nonlinear plot, in which events depend as much on the choices made by gods, serfs, and women as on the actions of the hero and the fighting men who accompany him. That is, it is often difficult to determine who or what is in charge, who or what should have the upper hand, who or what is to be trusted, and where exactly all this is heading.

Odysseus's wanderings, with all their inherent intrigue, compromise, detours, and struggle, nicely parallel the wandering we will embark upon now. It is also worth noting that for eight of the ten years on his "voyage" home to his beloved Penelope, Odysseus was the lover of someone or other.

The cyclical movement of trust and betrayal has taken me along a long, winding, and nuanced path in my own development. I know of no other aspect of relatedness that develops us more powerfully and brutally than that of trust and betrayal.

Now let's think about our terms.

---

*In respectful and loving memory of Dieter Egger, who died unexpectedly on 9 June 2010.

Trust: belief, confidence, expectation, faith, hope, comfort, consolation, fidelity, protection, assured reliance, dependence on something future or contingent. It is useful to distinguish between "primal," or unconscious, trust—the state before the "fall"—and "mature," or conscious, trust—the trust gained after we know the reality of betrayal.

Betrayal: an entire spectrum of meaning is associated with betrayal—from the conscious and intentional, such as revolt, mutiny, and treason to the unconscious and unintended, as in disclosure, unveiling, and revealing ("her blush betrayed her"). There are all kinds of things in between such as disobedience, violation, failure in duty, dishonesty, leading astray, abandonment, apostasy, treachery (cheating).

The perspective that has meaning for me assumes an entanglement between trust and betrayal and examines their necessity in human development. Each time you trust or are trusted, you face the possibility of betrayal. Each time you betray or are betrayed, you have the opportunity to embark on a journey toward new levels of trust. I would like to explore the developmental piece encapsulated in each experience of trust and betrayal.

Upon offering a prayer to Sophia, goddess of wisdom, to help me find the necessary links and pieces to bring something of worth to my topic and my audience, I had the following dream: *Dreamt of military drills and exercises. I had to find matching drills to do the work. I was looking for the matching drills because double-boring was necessary.* While this dream did not seem to bring light, good news, it did prove to be very helpful in my formation of ideas and feelings around the issues of trust and betrayal.

Trust and betrayal (as a dynamic system) is an intricate building block of human experience and psychological and emotional growth. Adults basically develop through and within relationships. These relationships include outer-reality ones such as love relationships, work relationships, family relationships, friend relationships, and professional relationships. They also include inner-reality ones such as the spiritual self, shadowy bits, the anima and animus (or perhaps better described as the inner feminine and inner masculine), and various other complexes, for instance parental introjects or hero and heroine images.

In my experience, a process weaves these two realities (inner and outer) throughout our whole life. The more consciously aware we are of this weaving process within ourselves, the more authentically we live the moral complexity of being human and the more honestly we move toward the one life we can call our own. When we do not weave the inner and outer realities together into one tapestry of our life, we tend to live splintered, part-existences and we betray something fundamental in ourselves, risking the danger of living an inauthentic life and resulting in what Eric Erikson called stagnation, the opposite of generativity.

This weaving process in relation to trust and betrayal is quite complex. It might help if we had a concrete example, so I have chosen the dilemma of bearing children in midlife, which I experienced myself.

EXAMPLE: THE NEED TO HAVE CHILDREN

I had always known in myself that I would have children, that I needed to have children, and that I would have them late in life. At age thirty-seven, I synchronistically met the father-to-be of my children on the train from Stadelhofen to Herrliberg. To make a long story short, at thirty-eight I was pregnant with Christopher. The father, Dieter, and I married, and at forty I had Catherine.

At that point in my life I was conscious that I was choosing Dieter to create a family with, a goal in life we both shared and both agreed to. I also knew that he was not the great love of my life. In my thinking, rational self I actually did not believe in such irrational stuff as finding "the love of one's life" or one's "soul mate." I had lived half of my life well enough without that. I reminded myself that I had significant friends and family and meaningful work and felt generally fine. I had met a man who, having given up on his dream of having a family, was now thrilled at the prospect. He was a good man, trustworthy, solid, responsible, and it felt right . . . enough.

I trusted my instinct and my personal inner need to have children. I trusted the synchronistic events that led to the real outer events and the physical reality of children. Aware of limitations in the relationship with my partner, I went ahead and said yes to a commitment that included marriage. Now what had happened psychologically and in terms of trust and betrayal?

At this point in time, was there betrayal? If so, of what or whom? Of myself or something in me? Of Dieter? Of our children? Of the marriage vows? Of my analysis and hard-won consciousness? Of our extended families and their fantasies? Of the collective and its prescriptions?

To complicate things, even while the children were young, I began having a repetitive dream of an inexplicable meeting with a man. Each time I had this powerful dream I tried to work with it: I tried to discover in Dieter this "meeting" I was having in my unconscious and *not* having in my conscious relationship. I tried with analysis to work on the integration of this image, which "knew" me like no other and brought me new life and energy. I tried in my outer world to use the power of this "meeting" to take new risks and face new challenges. I developed quite well in this way; that is, the dreams were very empowering and helpful as I worked out old father issues again in new ways. I even fell (vainly) in love during this time, recognized it had to do with this repetitive dream and its longing for growth, and worked it out for myself psychologically and emotionally. I was able to stay in my marriage, continue raising our children, and avoid getting into a deceptive relationship.

During these some eighteen years, what was happening psychologically and in terms of trust and betrayal? Was I trusting it to all work out? Was something being betrayed in terms of me, my husband, our family, the marriage vows?

Seven years ago, the heat ratcheted up a notch. Five years ago, the inner torment and outer dis-ease grew. Three years ago I knew that staying in the marriage, as it was, was killing me and that I had to make a change. We made a last-ditch effort, undertaking couples therapy. The longer that went on, the more sure I was of my decision to make a drastic change and move out. For my husband, everything at home was fine—he was just waiting for me to get better, get happy.

At this point in time, was this decision to make a physical change a move of trust or betrayal? Of myself, of Dieter, of our children, of the marriage?

And today, twenty-two years since the beginning of the story, I live apart from my husband, lead a very separate, fulfilled, and much happier life. We are still married, and neither one of us is interested in changing that status at this point. My perception is that we (Dieter and I) care about each other in similar, compassionate ways. Our daughter (now eighteen years old) lives with me during the school week and with him on weekends. Our son (now twenty) lives partly with his dad and partly with friends.

At the present moment, is this state of affairs a betrayal of myself, of Dieter, of the children, and/or of the marriage? It's complicated, isn't it?

MYTHOLOGICAL AND ARCHETYPAL FRAMING

I would like to explore with you now three mythological or archetypal aspects of trust and betrayal that can help us frame the complexity of the dynamic in adult relationships.

1. The Uroborus/Infant and Mother (natural trust and betrayal)
2. The Garden of Eden ("feminine" trust and betrayal)
3. Judas, Peter, and Christ ("masculine" trust and betrayal)

We each experience them all, in my view. Sometimes they are mixed together. I have some ideas about these patterns and would like to work on understanding the reasons or imperatives behind our actions, behaviors, and dilemmas and how they might help us learn about our own healing.

The Uroborus/Infant and Mother (Natural Trust and Betrayal)
The Uroborus is an ancient symbol depicting a serpent or dragon swallowing its own tail and forming a circle. The Uroborus represents the idea of primordial unity related to something existing in or persisting from the beginning with such force or qualities that it cannot be extinguished. Both Jung and Erich Neumann wrote about the archetypal significance of the Uroborus in the human psyche, Neumann emphasizing it as a representation of the pre-ego "dawn state" and depicting the undifferentiated infancy experience of both humankind and the individual child. For the individual child, it represents the primal state of bliss where all is provided and we are contained perfectly. This womb-like existence is usually experienced as a passive state of contentment. But then comes the shock of birth.

From the moment of conception, it is inevitable that we will be betrayed and that we will betray. Our first experience of betrayal, of being thrust out of the womb, leaves an indelible mark on our psyches and forms a recurring theme in our lives. We live with the illusion that this basic betrayal will be corrected in our love relationships. . . . There is no betrayal more wounding than the betrayal of love. It touches us in our most vulnerable spot, that of the helpless child who is totally dependent on another. This (vulnerable) child always emerges (in us) in any relationship where the possibility of trusting in another person exists.[1] Here we see nature at work, pure and simple. No moral lessons to be learned, just physical imperatives to be dealt with. Forced, amoral phase development. We experience this at birth, at death, and at many other times.

I had a very surprising experience with my own children that I think falls into this category of "natural betrayal." Christopher was just about four years old and Catherine was two. We were walking around our garden one day, when Christopher put his foot out and tripped his sister. I *immediately and without any conscious reflection* did the same to him. We were all shocked! To my astonishment, my motherhood capacity to automatically "set things right" had made itself known. There would have been very many other and better ways to deal with the situation, but this was somehow not about moral lessons, just physical fact! I was shocked at my own Nature as Mother, calling me to accept this amorality in myself and to deal with it in a related fashion with my children. This memory has kept me in touch with the ambivalence of my natural self and of nature herself and, I think, even of God itself.

The Uroborus also often represents self-reflection and the cyclical and continuous nature of life itself, illustrating that beginning comes out of ending and that endings of births are new beginnings. This aspect of the symbol is especially comforting when we betray or feel betrayed, and it can remind us that somewhere in those dark feelings of despair, new life is possible.

The Garden of Eden ("Feminine" Trust and Betrayal)
The biblical story of creation leads up to the primal act of disobedience, free will, and enlightenment *based on desire led by unconscious wisdom.* God charges Adam to tend the garden in which he and Eve live and specifically forbids him to eat from the Tree of Knowledge of Good and Evil, threatening him with death if he does so. The most clever of all the animals in the garden asks Eve, "Did God really say, 'You must not eat from any tree in the garden?'" Eve explains that they may eat from the trees, just not from the tree that is in the middle of the garden. She even adds to God's warning by saying that they may not *touch* that tree, lest they die. "You will not surely die," the serpent said to the woman, "for God knows that when you eat of it your eyes will be opened, and you will be like God, knowing good and evil." When the woman saw that the fruit of the tree was good for food and pleasing to the eye and *desirable for gaining wisdom,* she took some and ate it. She also gave some to her husband who was with her, and he ate it. At this point the two become aware of "good and evil," as is evidenced by their awareness that they were naked. God finds and confronts them, judges them for disobeying, and banishes them from the garden, lest they eat from the Tree of Life and live forever.[2]

Here we can also reflect on the trust-and-betrayal process as stemming from *desire from within and even encouraged by instinct and unconscious wisdom.* This is the following of a desire for more—for more potential, for more wisdom, for more humanity. And in so doing, we create an opening up of things, allowing them to flow differently than originally "planned."

To paraphrase James Hillman, "when Eden is over, life begins." He continues to describe the scene,

> The situation of primal trust is not viable for life. God and
> the creation were not enough for Adam; Eve was required,
> which means that betrayal is required. It would seem that the
> only way out of that garden was through betrayal and expulsion,
> as if the vessel of trust cannot be altered in any way except

through betrayal. We are led to an essential truth about both trust and betrayal; they contain each other. . . .

We are betrayed in the very same close relationships where primal trust is possible. We can be truly betrayed only where we truly trust—by siblings, lovers, spouses, not by enemies, not by strangers. . . . Trust has in it the seed of betrayal; the serpent was in the garden from the beginning. . . . Trust and the possibility of betrayal come into the world at the same moment. Wherever there is trust in a union, the risk of betrayal becomes a real possibility. And betrayal, as a continual possibility to be lived with, belongs to trust just as doubt belongs to living faith.[3]

When we find ourselves feeling and/or following such an inner desire, does it impact or imply anything in particular about the development of consciousness in the cycle of trust and betrayal?

I believe there is a specific requirement for integrating and living with the demands of this kind of truth. It has to do with the *purpose* of the desire to betray and the motivation driven by unconscious wisdom. My desire to, in fact the imperative to find the "inexplicable meeting" within myself and its subsequent impact on my outer relationships could not be denied. It would not let me rest with a "good-enough" solution that would have been easier for everyone to bear. The "good-enough" was keeping me from living a positive and essential potential. Guilt and forgiveness have to be contextualized within both realities, the inner and the outer.

Judas, Peter, and Christ ("Masculine" Trust and Betrayal)

Now let's turn briefly to another famous betrayal, the betrayal of Christ. What can we learn if we look at Christ and his betrayers, all of whom "fail" him, allowing him to be crucified and propelling him to fulfill his destiny?

Jesus predicts Judas's betrayal and Peter's denial of knowing him—and he even predicts his own destiny, asking God whether the cup could not be taken from him. (That is, "Can we not stop this particular part of the plan?") But he knows his destiny must be fulfilled. Unlike Eve, Jesus is not blinded by curiosity or desire or slyness. He remains conscious and even informs others they will betray, deny, and fail him. When told, Judas exclaims, "Surely not I, Rabbi?"[4] Peter declares, "Even if I have to die with you, I will never disown you."[5] We all know how the prophecy was fulfilled, and how necessary the betrayals were for its fulfillment.

Here we see what we could perhaps call a more conscious version of betrayal. It is based on something other than inner desire, something more tangible, like a principle, a complex, a fear, a plan, or a destiny. This kind of betrayal is for me like that of mutiny or treason and could even be associated with a change of conscious loyalty and sense of belonging. So there seems to be a conscious principle at stake here related to power and ideology.

When we find ourselves deciding and/or following such principles, does it impact or imply anything in particular regarding the development of consciousness in the cycle of trust and betrayal?

Let me give you another personal example, one that shames me greatly but one that I believe brings my point home. Catherine was always an active and strong-willed child. When she was three years old, she took it upon herself to secretly mix all of my perfumes, creams, and powders in a big mixing bowl with eggs. She then painted the walls and carpet with the amazing paste she'd made.

The fury that roared up in me when I found her was a mixture of how many hundreds of francs were in that paste, how I could not afford replacements, how this child just keeps breaking all the rules. I picked her up and literally threw her onto the mattress where she slept on the floor. In horror at myself, I dropped to my knees and crawled to her saying, "I don't get you, do I?" She shook her head slowly and sadly, "No." We were both crying. We gazed at each other intensely, and I said—half to her and half to myself—"I do now."

Deep within myself I promised never again to overlook the essence of this child's curiosity, intensity, and sense of purpose, never to not-see who and what she is, really. I asked for forgiveness from her, from myself, and from God, who had entrusted the care of this precious soul to me for some years. Accepting that forgiveness was possible meant that I had to change forever my way of being a mother to my children. I had to back up and meet them on their level. To admit that I didn't understand my daughter, I had to swallow my pride in having been a good mother up to that point. This required me to take on a part of my shadow as a true part of myself. It does not let me live split off from my inner shadow. Guilt and forgiveness have to be contextualized in relation to something and someone in the outer world.

In other words, the integration process is not exactly the same as the relational process, although the two belong together. I believe this is what my dream, relayed above, was trying to help me see: the coming-to-one's-truth needs to be approached as a "double-boring," that is, from two sides—from the side of personal integration and from the side of relationship.

There is a last and extremely important factor in the betrayal of Christ we have to look at, which is Jesus himself and his relationship to his fate. Jesus seems relatively at peace with his destiny throughout his life until the closing scenes in the Garden of Gethsemane, when he is overcome with sorrow: "My soul is overwhelmed with sorrow to the point of death."[6] Jesus then goes off by himself, falls with his face to the ground, and prays, "My Father, if it is possible, may this cup be taken from me. Yet not as I will, but as you will."[7] He repeats this a second and a third time. Even more powerful, on the cross his last words are, "My God, my God, why have you forsaken me?"[8]

Hillman describes it so poetically:

> The sorrow at the supper, the agony in the garden, and the cry on the cross seem repetitious of a same pattern, restatements of a same theme, each on a higher key, that a destiny is being realized, that a transformation is being brought home to Jesus. . . .
>
> He and the Father were one, until that moment of truth when he was betrayed, denied and left alone by his followers, delivered into the hands of his enemies, the primal trust between himself and God broken, nailed to the irredeemable situation; then he felt in his own human flesh the reality of betrayal and the brutality of Jahweh and His creation.[9]

To fulfill his destiny as God's son, it was not enough for Jesus to accept Judas's betrayal, Peter's denial, and the failure of the disciples (failure of duty in their falling asleep repeatedly). Jesus had to reach the point of despair and suffering in which he himself felt betrayed by his Father and his Fate/Plan. Then and only then was there transformation.

This is really bad news for you and me. It means we can't just theoretically agree to the idea of ego's death and rebirth as a way of eking out a bit of consciousness. For real psychological development, we have to continually, over and over again, live the pain and shame of being forced to face our true selves. We have to face betrayal by the Self, our self, our good intentions, our hopes, our dreams, our good deeds—just as we have face and accept the betrayal of others toward us.

Here we see destiny being realized, and unavoidably so. Being true to oneself means feeling betrayed, being betrayed, and betraying. You will notice an ambiguous point in all the stories: was God actually betrayed or were these developments in God's original plan? That is, did God set it up? Is God the ultimate traitor? If this is possible, why would it be so? Let's see if we can suggest an answer.

I have adapted Edward Edinger's well-known depictions of "The Psychic Life Cycle" to what I believe is the reparative cycle of trust and betrayal we are looking at.[10] Our task is complicated because we have to view the contents on several levels at one time: intrapsychically, as the betrayed and betrayer, and also interpersonally, as the betrayed and betrayer.

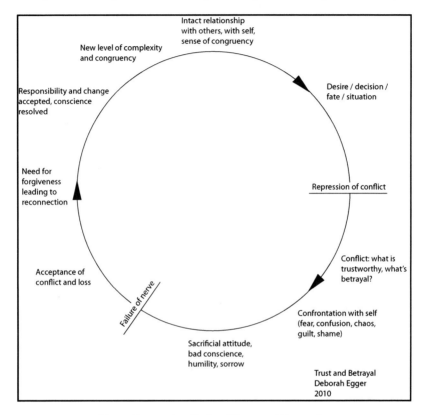

Fig. 1: Reparative Cycle of Trust and Betrayal.

Trust and betrayal are two aspects of relatedness that present a whole picture, tell a whole story. I link them together here because, psychologically understood, they represent two aspects of the same phenomenon of being humanly connected. They show a cyclical way of being with oneself and with an "other" or "others" that leads to deeper and more authentic relatedness.

1. Intact relationship with others, with self; sense of congruency.
2. Desire/decision/fate/situation.
3. Conflict/conflict repression. The broken promise or broken trust or broken security is simultaneously felt as a

disorienting chaos, and there can be an automatic or willed repression of the conflictual situation. Note that stopping the cycle due to repression of the conflict may be appropriate and/or necessary.

4. Confrontation with self/Self. What is trustworthy, what is betrayal, what is true, what is right, what is wrong? Fear, confusion, chaos, guilt, and shame reign.

5. Sacrificial attitude. Bad conscience, humility, sorrow. Does it matter whether the break of trust is conscious or unconscious? Whether it is willed or preordained, accidental, unintended, or natural—that is, coming from nature? Is there actually a way to discern which is which?

6. Failure of nerve. Turning back, undoing (at least for the moment) aborts the transformational process. Guilt cannot be borne and loses its context. This can also be a very appropriate break in the cycle of reparation.

7. Acceptance of conflict and loss. Taking responsibility for the complexity and the choice to go on. Guilt must be addressed within the whole context or all gains are lost.

8. Need for forgiveness, possibly on many levels. Forgiveness requires a change, which is the ultimate fruit of the transformation. The change can be in attitude, in behavior, in commitment, in relationship, in habit, in acceptance of something until now unknown and unwanted.

9. We reach a new level of complexity of humanness in our self, with others, and with the world, and a new sense of congruency is restored.

After we have experienced primal trust, we want to trust again. We look for it again, but the circle is not the same—we have inched up (or down) a notch. Betrayal that is acknowledged, suffered, and resolved does have a transformative effect on the individual. We can begin to see that betrayal is a necessary part of psychological development.

NOTES

[1] Jacqueline Wright, "Trust and Betrayal in Love," in *Jung Society Newsletter Articles* [C. G. Jung Society of Atlanta] (2006): 6–8, available at http://www.jungatlanta.com/articles.html.

[2] Genesis 3:1–12. This and all subsequent quotations from the Bible are from the New International Version Study Bible.

³ James Hillman, "Betrayal," in Hillman, *Loose Ends: Primary Papers in Archetypal Psychology* (Dallas, Tex.: Spring Publications, 1975), p. 66. Hillman's italics.

⁴ Matthew 26:25.

⁵ Matthew 26:35.

⁶ Matthew 26:38.

⁷ Matthew 26:39.

⁸ Matthew 27:46.

⁹ Hillman, "Betrayal," p. 69.

¹⁰ Edward F. Edinger, *The Sacred Psyche* (Toronto: Inner City Books, 2004), p. 83.

6

Self-Betrayal:
A Psychological Necessity?

Allan Guggenbühl

INTRODUCTION

The case seemed clear: the young woman had not acted on premeditation. After several intensive talks, her landlord concluded that his tenant was a victim of her own thoughtlessness and her artistic temperament. She had been sharing an apartment with three colleagues. As the apartment was rented officially in her name, she was responsible for collecting and paying the rent. She collected the money from her roommates quite conscientiously. The only problem was, she never transferred it to her landlord! She kept it for herself, later explaining that she had forgotten it in her purse and spent it unintentionally. Because the apartment building was family owned and not professionally managed, ten months went by before the landlord discovered the missing payments! As one can imagine, everyone was irritated. How could this young, talented singer deceive her roommates as well as her landlord? Finally, after long discussions, it was decided that she would be given another chance. The young woman's father came up with the missing sum and the landlord agreed to prolong her contract under the condition that she would analyze the roots of her absent-mindedness.

Consequently, she commenced therapy with me. The sessions with her were intensive. We reflected on her childhood, mulled over her relationship with her parents, and worked on transference issues. My impression was that we were progressing and managing to work on many previously unconscious topics and complexes. She was well acquainted with Jungian jargon. She considered herself an Aphrodite who demanded attention and admiration from her fellow humans. Her dreams confirmed this distinct pattern. The therapy was completed after one year, and I felt satisfied and convinced that she had been cured of her cheating tendency. Two months later, my assistant reported that a particular patient of mine was overdue with her payment. Guess who it was? Although the singer had collected the insurance, she had failed to transfer the money to my practice account.

Was this therapy a success? Or did I fail to get to the core of the singer's problem? Did I offer a stage for the reenactment of her pathology?

BASIC APPROACH

People seek therapy for many different reasons, such as to gain relief from stress, conflict, or the effects of trauma. Thus, as a therapist, I am expected to help my patients learn to independently manage their problems, to become better integrated in society and in their private lives, and to be happier people. From this perspective, the core purpose of therapy is *adaptation,* and we consider patients to be healed when they begin to function *normally.*

Of course, from a psychoanalytical perspective this definition is incomplete, for it reduces the psychotherapist to a functionary who adheres to society's norms and values and makes of these the guidelines for the therapeutic setting. In a Jungian approach, the goal of therapy further includes service to *psyche,* which entails self-reflection, seeking self-knowledge, and furthering the process of individuation.[1] By extension, Jungian therapists align themselves with the unconscious and with the symptom as something that is less to be cured than to be explored for its meaning. In this sense Jungians work like detectives, dedicated to investigating and deciphering the codes of the psyche and to trying to uncover its hidden motives.

Jungian therapy follows a distinct ritual, which is apparent, first, in the predetermined frameworks of time and place. Then there is privacy and the strictest confidentiality, which are paramount to the therapeutic undertaking. Indeed, in the eyes of the patient, the sessions should be perceived as akin to a sacred space in which the norms, values, and demands of everyday life have no bearing. The therapist's role is to be a trustworthy, attentive, nonjudging listener and interpreter, while patients are invited to freely elaborate their symptoms, histories, emotions, fantasies, dreams, wishes, slips of the tongue, body sensations, sudden pains, and any other manifestations that serve the therapeutic purpose. Sitting face to face, therapist and patient scan such material for clues that might help to create a new personal history, a new depth of self-understanding, and a new vision of life.

Trust needs to be underlined as a component of this "sacred space." It is also a prerequisite for successful therapy. Trust takes time and effort to build and can be demonstrated in many ways, such as through the therapist's demeanor, his or her choice of words, and the transference that he or she evokes. Trust is also conveyed through the therapist's adherence to professional standards. Only when trust is established—only when patients feel safe, comfortable, and convinced of the therapist's commitment to their well-being—can the intensive analytic dialogue begin.

SELF-IMAGE AS PROPAGANDA

Among the layers of psyche that soon become subject to therapeutic investigation is that of self-image: "Mutual respect and peaceful solutions are essential when dealing with adversaries," an adolescent client declared solemnly, at the same time proclaiming his innocence in a brawl in which one of the parties sustained serious injury. Of course, the other youngsters involved in the incident likewise described themselves as peace-loving and assuredly blameless beings who had never meant to attack and harm their contenders.

To those working with them, young offenders repeatedly reveal the problem of biased self-image. Recounting their violent engagements, they generally attribute to themselves acceptable, noble, or even more worthy motives while suspecting vile or heinous intentions behind the behavior of others. They claim their innocence and quite often perceive themselves as victims. They are convinced that their contribution to the fight was minimal and that their actions were examples of appropriate self-defense. When urged to reflect on their aggressive behavior, many young offenders ask, "Wouldn't you defend yourself too if you were insulted?"

This type of defense is widespread and common, not just among criminals. All of us—when we are caught doing something embarrassing or failing or engaging in wrongdoing—whitewash our actions instinctively, blaming others or the circumstances. The reasons for this reaction lie in the psychology of the self-image. Each of us has created such an image, through which we attribute to ourselves distinct strengths and weaknesses. We generally feel certain and correct in such self-knowledge. Unfortunately, our certainty is illusory, for it turns out that self-image does not mirror the whole personality.[2]

The way we see ourselves is simply not the way we actually are. Indeed, too much self-awareness can cause mental problems. For this reason, self-image is not designed to function as a factual mirror of our completeness. Instead, its chief duty is to keep us in balance—to keep us "up and going," confident and focused, free of excessive self-criticism and doubt. When working properly, self-image does these things by repressing a crippling consciousness of our abundant deficiencies, misbehavior, evil motives, shoddy plans, and other occurrences that contradict our consciously held beliefs and values.

Self-image is biased for another reason, which is to preserve the values that define our membership in specific groups, such as professional, social, and national groups. To sustain the sense of belonging, and lest we become alienated or ostracized, self-image functions to repress features that our surroundings condemn. For instance, who among us would risk openly endorsing corporal punishment in schools? Who would dare to loudly voice the conviction that women are unsuited for politics? Or that banning smoking in public places is pure hysteria? It would be impossible to confess to an erotic attraction to children or to admit to a marriage based on the partner's income bracket.

In short, we might say that self-image is designed to exclude shadow. The dilemma posed here is the patient's right to therapeutic understanding, on the one hand, and the therapist's responsibility to mistrust the propaganda, on the other. A patient might insist, "I always help conflicted parties get along with each other by presenting numerous possible solutions," while in reality creating a long record of malicious acts and a reputation for spreading trouble. In other words, what the therapist hears is distorted and is not enough to obtain an unbiased view.

THE EMPATHY TRAP

Empathy is considered a valuable psychotherapeutic tool that therapists use to see the world through their patients' eyes and experience it in their shoes. How does it feel to be bullied or cheated? To have been raped? Empathy is indeed important, for it enables us to get close to patients and understand the motives behind their actions. But there is a snag; empathy does not necessarily improve psychological understanding. On the contrary, the more empathy we mobilize, the greater is our loss of critical distance. The better acquainted we become with our patients, the more we assimilate their taboos, biases, and blind spots. Thus, empathy can lead to *mutual blindness,* making therapists akin to their patients in becoming unable to detect murky issues.

This mutual blindness is widespread. It has tainted psychotherapy's professional reputation and it has fueled the perception that psychotherapists are naïve and partial.[3] A case in point is that of the psychotherapist who forbade his patient to contact her parents because he was convinced they had abused her. Her parents were angered and insisted they were absolutely innocent. Despite the fact that he had never contacted them, the therapist remained adamant in his judgment, relying instead on his empathy and on his patient, whom he believed would never lie to him!

INNER-OUTER WORLD: A DECEPTIVE DISTINCTION

Another key notion informing psychotherapeutic work is the distinction between *inner and outer reality.* We define ourselves as beings who participate in external events, the happenings of our particular social group, and at the same time we keep a certain distance. We see, feel, and listen from a distinct personal position. Although we recognize our role in the drama around us, we sustain belief in our uniqueness and autonomy because we keep one foot planted in another realm: the inner world of private thought, feeling, and image. This inner world is perceived as an antidote to the outer world and as a solipsistic entity in the void of the universe. Thanks to the inner world, we are not just driven by base instinct, nor are we defined only by social codes. We can also achieve a personal stance that enables us to flourish.

However, this concept of two realities is deceptive because it assumes that the inner life is completely separate from the outer world and its pandemonium. Whereas self-reflection is said to allow us to discern a genuine inner voice, in reality our reflections and dreams do not arise in a free zone, independent of other influences. Rather, we remain more or less confined by the ego and other complexes while also being immersed in a sea of external ideas, emotions, actions, and thoughts that influence us from many angles. If we do not own up to this fact, we may fail in therapy to reflect on the implications of our embeddedness in culture, nation, and family. Our focus on sheer personal and inward experience, thought, and story can lead to desocialization and can even open a door to antisocial attitudes and feelings of moral superiority.

Moral superiority has begun to creep in when we perceive the world outside as being treacherous, vile, and full of evil while we attribute noble intentions to ourselves. Often we blame the usual suspects: big industry, politicians, "the system." We see ourselves as an antidote to a problematic society, tendering as proof the truth of our inner experiences and revelations. Yet in order to claim this exclusive position, we must offer an abridged version of our inner life, we must ignore the fact that as human beings who belong to a civilization we are always exploitive and irresponsible and are often unjust.

Fallacy in the "Self"

Jung conceived the "Self" as the unconscious and supraordinate center of the personality, the source that "knows better" when it sends us on paths that divert from our conscious goals and plans. Not being easily distracted by rules, trends, and fads, the Self keeps us rooted in what is psychologically good and important, conveying its meanings in archetypical images and symbols. The idea of the Self helps us recognize that our conscious motives may be only skin deep and prods us to be self-critical and questioning. To get at the deeper truths and goals, we strive for self-realization through the symbolic understanding of our dreams, images, and behavior.

The notion of the Self is a genuine contribution to psychology. By placing the knowledgeable center in the unconscious, Jung pointed to the necessity of *striving* for insight as well as the impossibility of gaining ultimate wisdom. The Self makes us curious, so the search for Self is a project that should be sustained.

The flip side is that the Self-encounter can lead to delusion—for instance, when we rely on numinous self-experience to legitimize decisions or attitudes that actually derive from egotistical motives. "I had a dream that said I should cancel my sister's party!" a woman exclaims and subsequently withdraws from making plans for the surprise celebration. While believing that she was following a message from the Self, this woman disregarded the reality of her own self-centeredness and disinclination to share the limelight with her sister. Similarly, a man was convinced of the Self's demand that he follow an artistic path and abandon his family for a bohemian life. In reality he was looking for a subterfuge to avoid the troubles that came with the duties of his domestic life. Thanks to the Self, we can cover up our selfishness and antisocial behavior.

Symptom Repertoire

In therapy, we seek to discover the causes of disturbance and distress by, among other ways, reflecting on the past, recalling our childhoods, and exploring the quality of our relationships with our parents. We develop stories that capture our symptoms and locate their roots, generally taking for granted our true representation of actual experience: "I was the victim of child abuse." "As a gifted child I was always subjected to my parents' ambitions." "I have low self-esteem because my father neglected me."

Again, we need to be aware of the potential for self-trickery. That which we hold to be true may be less a genuine product of self-reflection than an *unconscious and stereotypical* selection from the repertory of symptoms and diagnoses approved of by our psychotherapeutic culture.[4] Our culture at large also provides an approved repertory, which is subject to change according to popular taste. For instance, when "burnout" is *en vogue,* it readily supplies the rationale that our patients' suffering is caused by overengagement and the burden of excessive responsibility. Precisely because the respective criteria are part of the public discourse, they sound very convincing. However, popular explanations do not necessarily resonate for the soul, much less touch on the individual's deeper psychological issues or extend to the roots of his or her suffering.

THE GODS: A TRIP INTO DREAMLAND?

"I found out that the archetype of Aphrodite is awaking in me!" A common feature of analytical psychology is the attainment of insight that relies on a call to the gods.[5] Our clarity links us with Apollo, our cunning with Hermes, our craftsmanship with Hephaestus, our fierceness with Ares. We allude to our Greco-Judean heritage to grasp the dynamics and motives of our deeds. The core idea is that psyche is mirrored in myth and therefore that myth can reveal the patterns and destinies to which we unconsciously adhere.[6] Our turning to the gods may well open our eyes to self-imposed restrictions and inhibitions. Comparing our selves with the gods can also have the flattering effect of elevating life's banalities, such as when we attune ourselves to Aphrodite's call or heed Persephone's voice. To see the dreariness and intricacies of everyday life as part of an archetypical drama can be empowering and can motivate fresh starts.

On the other hand, the gods can detach us from the common-sense restraints of daily existence. Then we run off with a lover, ignoring the pleas of husband and family, because Aphrodite is stronger—or we answer Persephone by quitting a job as an accountant to become an inept painter. The quandary is that unlike the gods, we mortals are constrained by morals and social codes and are bound in national alignments, relationships, and families. Naturally, we cherish the dream of a limitless freedom in which our fantasies can be lived and our inner potential can be developed to the fullest. Yet reflecting on our everyday worries face to face with the gods bears the risk of escape into a dreamland, an exclusive zone that allows us to act irresponsibly, apolitically, and egocentrically. That which began as psychotherapy can transmogrify into spaced-out poetry sessions, therapist and patient dwelling in mutual infatuation with the divine. The consulting room becomes an isolated arena of grandiosity, in which two human beings lose sight of life's everyday dreariness and challenge, perhaps even convinced of their sharing a special relationship and understanding of the world out there.

IMPLICATIONS FOR OUR WORK AS PSYCHOTHERAPISTS

Self-image, empathy, inner and outer reality, and talk of the gods are both ingenious notions and stumbling blocks in Jungian psychotherapy. I do not devalue the system in asserting that we are obligated to remain aware of the inherent dangers these concepts bring to our work. On the contrary, the dangers result from the fact that Jungian psychotherapy, not content to offer superficial education and the mere abolishment of symptoms, dares to deal with the depth of soul. We concede that psyche, opposing the rules of logic, makes of us humans tricky, deceitful, multifaceted, creative, and paradoxical beings. Many well-delineated motivational concepts that fulfill our rational wish for clarity fail to implement the broader and deeper goals of Jungian psychotherapy.

A Triangular Relationship

To avoid falling into the empathy trap or overvaluing our patients' self-reporting, we must ground therapeutic work in a clear understanding of the psychotherapist's function. First of all, it is *not* primarily to offer a relationship between two equals. Rather, it is to engage in a *subservient occupation,* in which therapist and patient together deal with a third "other," namely, the unconscious. To put it slightly differently, psychotherapy binds us in a triangular relationship, whereby therapist and patient are mutually committed to work in the service of soul.

To serve soul means that rather than taking the lead or defining the goals, we as therapists recognize the limits of our knowledge. We understand that when we believe that we know, we may be off track. We realize that soul's intricate ways require our questions over and above our answers. Thus, we seek with our patients to mutually unearth the deeper motives that are concealed by ready-made, popular explanations. We strive together to discover meaning in the often-puzzling imagery of dream and fantasy. We struggle along *with* to understand our patients' experiences, perceptions, stories, dynamics, motives, and wishes. In essence, we provide assistance in a process in which the patients themselves are engaged—that is, in watching, hypothesizing, interpreting, and responding to the developments of soul.

The Therapist as Irritant

Appreciation of our patients is important. Understanding them, however, does not require us to agree with their views, thoughts, and stories. Indeed, recognizing the difficulty of distinguishing between fact and fiction and acknowledging the likelihood of our succumbing to deception, our task is to *query*—perhaps especially those accounts that sound most convincing. Unlike a compassionate partner, we must sustain reasonable doubt and suspicion, for to remain in consent is to endanger the therapeutic process.

We might conceive of ourselves as necessary *irritants,* allowing ourselves enough leeway to make vexing comments and interpretations. "Well, maybe you *have* failed" could be an apt therapeutic response to a patient complaining about his boss's dissatisfaction with his work. Risking the angry backlash, we appreciate the difficulty and challenge of assuming this role. Of course, we would do well to explain it to our patients, who deserve to know in advance that their therapist can be expected to materialize as a contrarian from time to time. Also, acting as an irritant is constructive only when the relationship is based on trust; that is, when our patients are convinced of our therapeutic dedication to their psychological processes.

The Array of Archetypes

As previously mentioned, therapy in general risks the possibility that we will resort to culturally approved explanations that frame our patients' symptoms in stereotypical terms, with the result that we may fail to reach psyche's depths and the roots of suffering. When we employ an archetypal perspective, we draw closer to the language and life of soul. Our work with the figures of myth and literature expands the array of explanatory possibilities, also improving our ability to reflect beyond cultural norms and prejudices. For instance, the death of Pan can be introduced to illuminate the dynamics of passion, or Shakespeare's Falstaff can throw light on the value of self-irony and humor in the face of power and hypocrisy. We speak more directly to soul—and thus better support deep self-reflection—when we can share with patients our sense that their unconscious pursuit of certain archetypes is engendering their culturally unacceptable or morally inadequate behavior. One can be driven by the Trickster, for example, or besotted by Aphrodite. In this sense, Jungian therapy goes beyond popular explanation to seek diagnosis and prognosis, as it were, in the client's archetypical background and cultural heritage.

THE IMPORTANCE OF BETRAYAL

Psychotherapy usually begins with virtuous intentions that include trust, sincerity, and wholeness and with high-quality goals for the patient-therapist relationship. We search for mutual understanding, strive for empathy, attune ourselves to emotions, and listen to body sensations. All the while, we claim to engage in a mode of dialogue that differs from that which we find with friends and other intimates. Yet, as shown before, the therapeutic relationship is influenced and may be manipulated by shadow motives and complexes. Partners in therapy can become deceived by self-images or deluded in mutual infatuation. As therapists, we must remain vigilant. In our occupation, to be sincere is to also be suspicious.

At the same time, we must concede that betrayal, while it generally takes place unconsciously, is part of every relationship, including the psychotherapeutic. Earlier, I alluded to this in suggesting that the inherent one-sidedness of self-image serves to thwart the mental problems that can arise when one has too much self-awareness. The corollary would be that betrayal and self-betrayal are sometimes necessary to preserve sanity. In other words, because our egos can become fractured by the attempt to contain the enormity of the shadow, it can be sane to remain blind to our omissions, malicious motives, and other dark matters.

In health, we are generally neither motivated by nor desirous of encounters with our shadows. Generally speaking, we are better-functioning people when we *avoid* murky issues.[7] It is an illusion to believe that our pursuit of self-knowledge invariably leads to greater personal satisfaction and a more fulfilled life. As long our surroundings do not prompt questioning, deep reflection is unnecessary. Life is easier and often we are more productive, both personally and professionally, when the intricate questions go unasked.

This state of affairs leads again to the question of the role and duty of the psychotherapist. As Jungians, we find ourselves in a difficult position. Naturally, we are loath to forfeit our conscious intentions in favor of a cynical stance. We wish to believe in the good of our occupation, the sincerity of our aims, and our ability to help the patient reach an improved self-understanding. We have to realize, though, that our possibilities are limited and that we are not entirely in command of ourselves. Therapeutic work is full of traps and entails an indeterminate struggle with delusions, infatuations, and deceptions.

As therapists, we should sustain doubt about what is happening in therapy and in ourselves. Indeed, the feeling that we have succeeded in therapy can often be a sign that we are completely locked off and detached from unconscious motives. On the other hand, the feeling of failure can be a sign of success. One of the most pressing occupational and moral struggles might emerge in our attempt to resolve these questions: When is it right to assist our patients in their self-encounter and endeavor to disclose hidden motives? And when is it better to support our patients' repression—their self-betrayal, if you will—because it is a necessity that enables them to keep their lives in reasonable balance?

NOTES

[1] Jolande Jacobi, *The Way of Individuation,* trans. R. F. C. Hull (New York: Harcourt, Brace & World, 1967).

[2] David Livingstone Smith, *Why We Lie: The Evolutionary Roots of Deception and the Unconscious Mind* (New York: St. Martin's Press, 2004).

[3] Elaine Showalter, *Hystories: Hysterical Epidemics and Modern Media* (New York: Columbia University Press, 1997).

[4] Ethan Watters, *Crazy Like Us: The Globalization of the American Psyche* (New York: Free Press, 2010).

[5] Friedemann Wieland, *Die ungeladenen Götter. Selbsterfahrung mit Mythen und Märchen* (München: Kösel, 1986).

[6] Verena Kast, *Paare* (Stuttgart: Kreuz, 1984).

[7] Allan Guggenbühl, *Anleitung zum Mobbing* (Oberhofen: Zytglogge, 2008).

Grandparents: Between Grandness and Betrayal

Joanne Wieland-Burston

As we are meeting up here in the Swiss Alps, I would like to begin this excursion into the realm of grandparents with a touch of local color. I am thinking of one of the most well-known grandparents in literary history, Heidi's grandfather, from the children's book *Heidi,* written in 1880 by Swiss author Johanna Spyri.

As most of you will probably remember, Heidi is sent to live in the Alps in a little place near Maienfeld—about 90 minutes' drive east of Gersau, the venue for Odyssey 2010. She is to live with her grandfather, a recluse with a bad reputation. Heidi's Aunt Detie feels it is the grandfather's duty to take care of the little girl. I am sure you can well remember how sweet, loving, and kind Heidi's grandfather was to her and how devoted Heidi was to the old man. What you probably will not remember are the rumors about the grandfather's history and the way this history is recounted. In the first chapter, Detie—Heidi's previous caretaker—gives in to her friend Barbie's insistent questioning and tells the grandfather's story: he had inherited all of his parents' money, spent it carelessly, and then went off to Italy to serve in the Neapolitan army, where he supposedly killed a man in a brawl. When he returned to his village many years later, the people were unfriendly to him, so Grandpa retreated to a little place in the mountains where he lived an isolated life as a grumpy old man.

Now just imagine what would happen if little Heidi should hear this story! This was also a potential problem for Aunt Detie, who, before beginning her account, "glanced round to make sure that Heidi was not within earshot."[1] Of course it would not be good for Heidi to hear the story (whether it is rumor or truth), as she is going to be sent to live with this man. Yet her aunt's caution is not an unusual phenomenon: grandchildren are often intentionally kept in the dark about embarrassing stories from their grandparents' past. The shadow of the grandfather archetype seems to be especially difficult to accept. Why this is so and what effect it can have on the grandchildren are the central points I shall be concerned with here.

GRANDPARENTS' SHADOWS

I have been working in Germany as an analyst for over twenty years now. Many times I have worked with and otherwise met people whose grandparents' participation in the National Socialist period has been unclear: it was kept secret or was even lied about. I believe that not only a dark Nazi shadow but also secrecy and deceit about the past have a definite effect on the descendants' sense of identity. It is in light of this particular history that I shall explore the topic of grandparents—their special grandness and what the discovery of their shadow can mean for their grandchildren's identities. The revelation of this shadow can feel like betrayal, especially when the grandparents have concealed who they were and what they did during the war. The problem lies in the discrepancy between the image the grandchildren cherish and the shadow that they subsequently either discover or suspect. How they manage to live with this betrayal depends on each individual's capacity to deal with chaos or the shadow: by consciously suffering and integrating it; by denying, rejecting, or rationalizing it; or even by identifying with it. Or—as most often is the case—by splitting it off.

I should add here that there are two grandmothers in the Heidi story. Both are caring and lovable. One of them is forceful and helpful; the other one is blind and rather helpless. Neither grandmother's past is mentioned in the book; we do not know whether they were tainted in any way or not. This absence of a past corresponds with my own observations: I have never yet met a person in Germany who knows or speaks of a grandmother with a shameful past, although there is historical proof of women having been active and cruel in the Nazi system. These grandmothers' shadows seem to be even more taboo than the grandfathers' shadows.

In the second part of my essay I shall deal more directly with the issue of how national history (either transmitted or hidden by grandparents) can influence the development of personal identity.

THE GRANDPARENT ARCHETYPE

I must begin by clarifying the elements that belong to the archetype of grandparents. What comes to mind right away is the kind, loving, and caring way that grandparents generally relate to their grandchildren. (Is it perhaps because of the promise of immortality that grandparents see in the children of their offspring?) Family photographs often bear witness to the positive mirroring that we know is so important for child development. Grandchildren respond accordingly, with love, caring, and trust. Grandparents are also looked up to: they are venerable. Their long life experience contributes to the high esteem in which they are held. This unique mutual love and admiration is really something very special. Of course, there is tremendous idealization going on here, on both sides. This is obviously echoed in the English word "grandparents," as well as the German "*Grosseltern*" and the French "*grands-parents.*"

The ubiquity of this archetypal phenomenon is confirmed on the Internet, where numerous websites are devoted to grandparents and to grandparents' photographs of their grandchildren. There is also the rather recent celebration of Grandparents' Day, instituted in the United States in 1978 by President Jimmy Carter; it takes place on the first Sunday after Labor Day. In France the Fête des Grand-mères (Grandmothers' Day) has been celebrated since 1980 on the first Sunday in March. In Italy the Festa dei Nonni e Nipoti (Grandparents' and Grandchildren's Day) is on October 2nd. Bulgaria, Poland, Turkey, and Moldavia have also followed suit and celebrate their grandparents on given days.

In analytical practice we witness the importance and durability of the love and care of grandparents, especially when compassionate relationships with parents have been lacking. This early positive relationship often provides the only possible basis for a positive transference to the therapist, something that is so essential for the work. To mention one example: a woman in her thirties grew up with a physically and verbally abusive father and a weak and apparently psychologically blind mother. But she had the good luck to have been cared for regularly by her maternal grandmother. This old woman provided the little girl with the only stable, positive, caring memories of her childhood. For example, she could sleep calmly on the couch while Grandma prepared lunch in the next room. Sleeping was otherwise fraught with fear, as the child lived in constant dread of her father's nightly visits and abuse. This deeply traumatized girl grew up to be an extremely disturbed person, anorexic and confused about her sexual identity; she dissociated and cut herself frequently. Basically distrustful of people, she fought the therapists in the clinics she had been admitted to on several occasions because of suicidal tendencies. Our work was long and difficult, but one essential aspect helped us along the way and was a cornerstone for our successful result: my client was extremely reliable and trusting in our one-to-one relationship. I am sure that this trust was based on her early experiences with Grandma.

But besides the love and caring grandparents can offer, there is another significant aspect of the archetype: the role of grandparents as living representatives of the ancestors. German etymology supports this view: the Middle High German word *An,* meaning "grandfather," is the etymological root of *Ahn,* meaning ancestor. The word for grandson, *Enkel,* is the diminutive of *An* and refers to the fact that, as in many other cultures, the Germanic tribes considered the grandson to be the reincarnation of the grandfather (they often named the child after his grandfather).[2] Grandparents are held in high esteem because they link their descendants to the past and to the spiritual and godly realms. Tribal societies that celebrated ancestor cults are exemplary in this respect. In ancient Rome, the spirits of the dead were worshipped as Manes, or the souls of the dead. Ancient China practiced the custom of ancestor worship. The Mayan creation myth, the Popol Vuh, considered Xpiyacoc and Xmucané, who were grandparent gods, to be creators of the world. And the people of Teotihuacan who predated the Mayans imagined their creator god as an old man, Teoteohotl.

When we think about it, we realize that many Christian images portray God as an old man with a beard—including Michelangelo's famous God of creation in the Sistine Chapel and William Blake's Christian-inspired mythical figure Urizen. These examples all coincide with popular religious ideas that conceive of God in this way. The nineteenth-century commercial image of Santa Claus probably ties in here: millions picture a jolly old man with a big white beard who is kind to children as having some kind of a connection with the spiritual realm.

Thus, we have the image of grandfathers as wise old men who even created the world. We also have the experience of grandfathers passing down tradition (religious, spiritual and/or cultural). Grandparents—as well as parents—customarily transmitted to their descendents social, religious, and moral values as well as practical knowledge. The boat builder who taught his son and grandson his handicraft was helping to ensure that following generations would have the means of survival. In such societies the old were considered knowledgeable, wise, and deserving of respect. Filial piety was a basis for social functioning. In periods of history when social conformity was the rule and provided a secure basis for society, the task of transmitting culture—traditional, collective values and rituals—was of utmost importance. This phenomenon adds to the grandness of grandparents.

Idealization combined with a special loving relationship makes grandparents potentially powerful figures and role models. The impact grandparents have on the individual depends on various factors having to do with family situation and the psychological makeup of those involved. However, and this is the essential point, the archetypally given potential to influence the development of the child's identity through unconditional mutual love and an ancestral position is basic to the process. I am thinking here of a client who became a famous cook. When he was a child, his mother beat him regularly. His father worked hard but never stood up for his little boy or showed him how to stand up to his mother. This father was rarely present, either physically or emotionally. However, my client's grandmother often took care of him, and she spent a large part of their time together cooking with him. Grandparents as models can significantly influence the development of their grandchildren's identity.

GRANDPARENTS TODAY

But generally speaking, do grandparents today continue to transmit culture, traditions, and values? Do they still act as role models? Today collective values are no longer absolute truths to be respected and followed. The young are often better informed than the old; grandchildren rather than grandparents master the technical means of communication. The grandparent relationship is changing in other ways, too. In contemporary Western society, where in many households both parents work outside the home for wages, grandparents often play the role of caregivers. In fact, the Italian word for grandfather, *nonno,* means someone who cares for a child. However, when one asks grandparents how they see their role, they mention storytelling as well as babysitting.

Storytelling can help build a foundation for grandchildren, giving them a sense of identity: knowing where they come from can provide them with a sense of rootedness during a period of our history when roots are no longer a natural given. If we consider storytelling as a means of transmitting collective memory and traditional values, we are faced with a major psychological question: What effect might grandparents' stories and values have on their grandchildren today? And when the grandchildren are left in ignorance of grandparents' real history, how does this affect them? As we know, the psyche is as deeply (if not more deeply) moved by fantasy as it is by reality. For grandchildren, ignoring what grandparents actually did and instead harboring lively fantasies about their unknown past can be more formative and more harmful than knowledge of the truth.

BETRAYAL

What do I mean by betrayal in this context? With a pinch of poetic license, I can locate it in Little Red Riding Hood, who discovers not the grandmother she expected to find lying in bed but one with very different traits. When Red Riding Hood sees the wolf in Grandma's clothes, she innocently remarks on the changes. We can say that she is on the verge of discovering that Grandmother can also be a frightening wolf in disguise. She has hidden these aspects of her personality up to this point in the story. Grandmother is not what she seemed to be. Thus, the fairy tale provides an image of the betrayal that transpires when grandparents are not merely the people they appear to be or pretend to be what they are not. They lie about their life history by omission or even explicitly, by falsifying their stories. In so doing, they also betray their function as transmitters of history, leaving their grandchildren in the dark about their true identities and life experiences.

The tipping of an archetype into its opposite is not unusual; the more extremely one end of the scale is lived, the more extremely the opposite must at some time appear. The exceptionally loving figure can become the exceptionally wicked one, like Kali, the destructive mother who is at the opposite end of the archetypal scale from the birth-giving mother. A reversal can always occur when an ideal is disappointed: this is unavoidable during the normal course of development. There is also the inevitable betrayal of abandonment when grandparents, who can still be so desperately needed for their warmth and love, die. And then there is the betrayal when grandparents fail to fulfill their archetypal service—when they are anything but models to be emulated, when they are neither wise nor morally upright, when they do not transmit important knowledge or values.

I shall give here a few brief examples of the influence of grandparents' betrayal of grandchildren. A young woman came to her first analytical session to tell about the shock she had felt when she was given her maternal grandmother's cookbook. She had known the grandmother as a very kind old woman who had told stories of the family's terrible suffering from famine and other hardship during the Second World War. Leafing through the cookbook, the granddaughter found the following recipe: "Wartime cake: 12 eggs, 2 pounds of butter, 500 grams of flour, 2 pints of cream . . ." I need not continue giving away the secret family recipe for this luxurious cake. It demasked the grandmother and the family and created turmoil in the young woman: her sense of identity as the descendant of a family who had suffered during the war was shaken by this new image of relative prosperity. The discrepancy between this image and the old image that had been passed down to her felt just too great to bear.

In a similar vein, a young woman sought analysis when she discovered some old papers in the cellar that betrayed the fact that her beloved and caring grandfather had been a member of the S.S. (Schutzstaffel), Hitler's special military organization, which was declared responsible for crimes against humanity at the Nuremberg Trials. What did this discovery mean for her? Her own identity as the granddaughter of a kind and loving grandfather felt completely challenged, if not destroyed. It just did not fit. And why did he keep the truth from her? If her grandfather had been an S.S. man, what was she? This split in her image of her grandfather was unbearable; for her it meant a split in her own personality. For quite a while after this discovery she tried to explain the disjunction by telling herself that if Grandpa had really been an S.S. man (which she continued to doubt, despite the documents she had found), he must have worked benevolently in this position, caring for soldiers in a military hospital. Otherwise the truth of her grandfather's involvement was unbearable. Imagining a wolf in Grandpa's stead was impossible for her.

A little boy in primary school was told about the Shoah (the Hebrew word meaning "catastrophe" and, I feel, the correct term for what is popularly called the Holocaust). He went home, obviously perturbed, with the question, "Grandpa wasn't a Nazi, was he, Mommy?" Imagining that the grandfather he had never known might have been a villainous figure was horrifying for the boy. Behind his question, it appears, was a desire to dissociate the image of evil from himself and his family.

Opa war kein Nazi is the fitting title of a book published in 2002 that describes the results of a research project at the University of Hanover.[3] An abbreviated version of the research findings appears in the English monograph entitled *Grandpa Wasn't a Nazi*.[4] On the basis of 142 interviews, including forty conversations with families, and analysis of 2,535 stories, the authors came to the conclusion that grandfathers generally did not reveal their Nazi past. In the few cases when they did, the grandchildren tended to ignore such revelations and cling instead to their images of good, innocent grandparents who were victims of the war, having suffered hunger and bombings by the English and Americans as well as rape and torture by the Russians. The grandmothers mentioned in this research are all perceived to have had no connection with the Nazi atrocities.

Another interesting fact noted in the book is that different generations had different reactions to family involvement. Parents' involvement in the war seems not to be as difficult to digest as grandparents' involvement. I have also observed this phenomenon in therapy. It may be due to the fact that the relationship with parents is more contentious than the relationship with grandparents. Parents' shadows are hard to bear, but they are part of the package. Learning to recognize them—and, ultimately, to accept them—is part of the developmental process. This is definitely not the case with grandparents, who are most often idealized. Their archetypal position as ancestors definitely contributes to their idealization and to their grandchildren's unwillingness to recognize and accept their shadows.

NATIONAL HISTORY AND NATIONAL IDENTITY

The further question I am interested in probing here is the effect of grandparents' betrayal—either by omission or through conscious deception—on the development of their grandchildren's national identity. Identity is composed of various complexes that include both personal and collective facets, and it is by association with these that we come to define ourselves. In the very personal realm, identity builds on aspects such as our looks, our likes and dislikes, our clothing, our gender, our abilities, and our strengths and weaknesses. Then there is the collective realm, in which identity is generally built on our association with family, neighborhood, social class, ethnic and religious groups, and nation and national history.

During our particular period in history, however, nationality often seems to play a relatively minor role in the building of identity in a conscious and positive sense. Nationality seems to be most important when we are traveling abroad, and perhaps also when we are rooting for our national soccer team. Indeed, young people in Germany tend to identify themselves most readily and proudly as Germans when their teams are playing in international sport events. But they have far more difficulty when it comes to identifying with their country's history. The topic of national history in Germany is practically always burdened with shame, a feeling that may be conscious or may reside deep in the unconscious. The result is not only a disturbance of personal identity for many people in Germany, but also an ambivalence or split in their sense of national identity.

I personally experienced this phenomenon the most painfully during the time of the Vietnam war. I was a teenager when my family and I moved to Canada. It was the 1960s, and the world outside the United States was voicing loud condemnation of the horrors that the American army was wreaking on the population of Vietnam. It felt to me, transplanted to Canada, as if my country and I were being damned. Being identified with America's shadow did not make my teenage years easier, to say the least. Similarly, not all Italians are eager to be identified with the Mafia or even with their present head of state, Silvio Berlusconi.

With the advent of the European Union, the question of national allegiances and national identity may, with time, become obsolete. Future generations may find this to be an advantage, but they too will develop their own collective complexes, if not from their sense of belonging to a country then from their sense of being Europeans. Without grandparents or other ancestors to tell stories about pre–European Union times, the collective identity-building process will be a continental matter instead of a national one.

CONCLUSION

It is especially in Germany that I have encountered descendants of those who performed the Nazi horrors, and these descendants find it extremely difficult to identify with their native country. As the University of Hanover study mentions and as I have personally witnessed, the descendants often have the impression that the Nazi perpetrators all died off at the end of the war. Of course this is not true, but very few are informed about or are able to acknowledge their families' direct involvement in Nazi horrors. Grandchildren most often tend to split off feelings of shame and guilt that stem from fantasies about their grandparents' acts and beliefs during the Shoah. This necessarily leads to a rejection of certain aspects of identity that hampers the development of a mature and stable personality.

In analytical work I hope to help the individual find a sense of identity that can retain the experience of the "grand" of grandparents without having to deny the shadow aspects, to experience both the positive and the negative dimensions of this archetype. Ideally, and with time, guilt and shame about the past can be replaced by a sense of responsibility for the future. But the enormity of the National Socialist shadow is in such stark contrast with the Santa Claus–like realm of grandparents that the defenses are immense. And this is understandable. Coming to accept the reality of the shadow—allowing for a process of grief and suffering, of mourning—is always an unavoidable step on the path of individuation. And although the wartime generation is slowly dying off, the unconscious inheritance continues. The ability of these following generations to suffer consciously the betrayal of their ancestors will be crucial for their sense of identity and necessary for the development of their capacity for trust and relatedness in their personal lives and in the world.

NOTES

[1] Johanna Spyri, *Heidi,* trans. Eileen Hall (London: Penguin Books, 1956), p. 10.

[2] Das Wissenschaftliche Rat der Dudenredaktion, *Duden, Band 7. Etymologie. Das Herkunfts Wörterbuch der deutschen Sprache* (Mannheim, Vienna, Zurich: Duden Verlag, 1963), pp. 15, 138.

[3] Harald Welzer, Sabine Moller, and Karoline Tschuggnall, *Opa war kein Nazi: Nationalsozialsmus und Holocaust im Familiengedächtnis* (Frankfurt am Main: Fischer Taschenbuch Verlag, 2002).

[4] Harald Welzer, *Grandpa Wasn't a Nazi: The Holocaust in German Family Remembrance,* trans. Belinda Cooper, based on Harald Welzer, Sabine Moller, and Karoline Tschuggnall, *Opa war kein Nazi: Nationalsozialsmus und Holocaust im Familiengedächtnis* ([New York]: American Jewish Committee, 2005), www.memory-research.de/cms/download.php?id=2.

8

Trust and Betrayal: Four Women under Jung's Shadow

Judith A. Savage

INTRODUCTION

E arly in the twentieth century, women from all over the world began a pilgrimage to Zurich and Dr. Jung's consulting room. Jung's concept of individuation and his recognition that the soul was not the exclusive property of men had ignited in them a search for self-discovery and the hope of a life beyond the traditional roles allowed women at the time. Hélène Preiswerk, Frank Miller, Sabina Spielrein, and Antonia Wolff exemplify the many women who were present early in the history of Jungian psychology. Though each was enriched by their contact with Jung, his powerful *mana* personality and the patriarchal privilege and Victorian notions of femininity prevalent at that time did as much to obscure their identities as to enhance them.[1]

Each of these women was a luminous screen upon which Jung projected his ideas and theories. Hélène Preiswerk gave form to Jung's notions of the occult, Frank Miller to the reality of the mythopoetic unconscious. Sabina Spielrein identified the dark, regressive, and destructive elements of the unconscious, and Antonia Wolff embodied the curative and healing anima. Were their accomplishments greater than those of Freud or Jung? No doubt they were not, but because the issue of their psychological and historical betrayal has not been fully explored, the full truth about their contributions has not yet emerged.

These four women shared a mediumistic quality, and their entrancing natures must have attracted Jung just as the hysterical woman patient had captured the collective imagination of psychiatry at the turn of the twentieth century.[2] Women's delicate sensibilities and their mysterious bodies were deeply associated with a feminized notion of the unconscious, and they embodied the opposing "other" to the heroic and positivistic masculine psyche of the period. According to Susan Rowland, perhaps Jung was attracted to their mediumistic personalities precisely because he desired to become a medium himself. She stated: "In truth, he did [become a medium], especially in the spiritualist writing of *Seven Sermons to the Dead.*"[3] Jung's *Red Book* is another example of visionary experience, one in which he visited the world of the interior unconscious much like the medium encountered the spirits of the dead. James Hillman also imagined that Jung utilized mediumistic processes and was, for a time, dependent upon the medium's skills until he had acquired them for himself: "We may surmise that an endogamous aspect had perhaps been carried by Hélène, his cousin on his mother's side. . . . It is implied that Jung later integrated the gift of his endogamous anima, no longer requiring that it be experienced through projective rapport with Hélène."[4]

As the subjects of Jung's research, these women were his human canvas, and the issues of trust and betrayal were played out upon the interpersonal field between male analyst and female subject. What exactly is the nature of Jung's betrayal of these women and how might it have influenced analytical psychology? What is the human cost of exposing subjects to public humiliation or knowingly participating in concealing or distorting their histories?

Christine Marks has noted that for turn-of-the-century doctors, one of the fascinations of the hysterical woman was the "spectacle of a self without boundaries."[5] In contrast, Jung offered the metaphor of the *vas bene clausum*, or the well-sealed vessel. In alchemy, the *vas bene clausum* was a frequently mentioned precautionary measure. Jung wrote that it was "the equivalent of the magic circle. In both cases the idea is to protect what is within from the intrusion and admixture of what is without, as well as to prevent it from escaping."[6] For Jung, the contents of the *vas* were *imaginatio,* "the active evocation of (inner) images *secundum naturam,* an authentic feat of thought or ideation, which does not spin aimless and groundless fantasies . . . just [to] play with its objects, but tries to grasp the inner facts."[7] These precious contents were to be protected by boundaries in the analyst-client relationship.

It is precisely within the *vas bene clausum* that Jung's betrayal occurred and trust was violated. Whenever the seal of the *vas* is breached, it constitutes an alchemical failure, corrupting the work. Such betrayal in the analyst-client dyad constitutes what philosopher Judith Butler called the eradication of a human life. She reminds us "how easily a human life is annulled" and, with Emmanuel Levinas, insists that all ethics begins with "an apprehension . . . of the precarious life of the Other." According to Levinas, "Those who remain faceless . . . authorize us to become senseless before the lives we have eradicated. . . . Certain faces must be admitted into public view, must be seen and heard for some keener sense of the value of life, all life, to take hold."[8] These four stories reveal such betrayal. These women became "faceless" within the historical record, their identities distorted in the name of science.

HÉLÈNE PREISWERK

In *Psychiatric Studies,* Jung described a case he had under his "observation between 1899-1900"; he titled his study "A Case of Somnambulism in a Girl with Poor Inheritance (Spiritualistic Medium)."[9] In its foreword Jung wrote in a way that would lead readers to infer that his observations had occurred in a medical setting: "I was not in medical attendance upon Miss S.W.[;] unfortunately no physical examination for hysterical stigmata could be made."[10] The truth is, the patient was never under medical observation. She was Jung's maternal cousin, Hélène Prieswerk, and she was fifteen years old when Jung wrote his case study. The first séance Hélène conducted had actually taken place in 1895, when Jung was nineteen and his cousin-subject was only thirteen—not between 1899 and 1900, or when she was "15½," as described in *Psychiatric Studies.*[11] There are other inaccuracies in Jung's account that inflate his standing in the medical profession. Though he was only a first-year medical student, Jung described the research as occurring "towards the *end* of my medical training."[12] In addition, these "experimental séances" were not conducted in a hospital or clinic but in the living room of the Jung family home with only his cousin-subject, their mothers, their sisters, and one or two of their childhood friends present.[13]

Hélène, nicknamed Helly, was the eleventh of fifteen children. Her paranormal activity included the turning of tables and speaking in other voices and languages. Under trance she channeled her deceased grandfather and a figure she called Ivenes, whom she identified as a Jewish woman from the time of King Solomon. Jung was impressed by the difference between the young Helly and the more mature personality of Ivenes. Susan Rowland noted that the character of Ivenes, "contain[ed] the germ of Jung's distinct theories by suggesting that spirits are psychic phenomena. This idea indicates that parts of the unconscious mind work independently of the ego."[14] Under trance, Helly traveled to Mars and described it in detail.

In March 1900, Helly described "the structure of the mystic world in a series of seven circles."[15] Her revelations of this world foreshadowed Jung's 1916 mandala-like artwork, which he called *Systema mundi totius*, "[the] first mandala I constructed . . . wholly unconscious of what it meant."[16]

Many in the Jung family believed that young Helly had a crush on her older cousin Carl and that her desire to please him had motivated her trances.[17] Deirdre Bair writes that Hélène told her friend Emmy Zinsstag, "Carl wants to explore the soul and the hereafter. I've chosen to help him in this exploration. That's my destiny which makes me happy."[18]

Hélène Preiswerk's adolescent life was forever encapsulated in her role as Jung's first research subject. Although Jung gave her a pseudonym in his 1902 thesis, "On the Psychology and Pathology of So-Called Occult Phenomena," he revealed so much of her family history that her identity was exposed. For the rest of her life, Hélène struggled to be perceived as someone beyond Jung's "Girl [of] Poor Inheritance" whose "education was deficient," who was "somewhat rachitic . . . with a peculiar penetrating look," who had descended from a family with a history of waking hallucinations.[19] Jung's recitation of his subject's poor genetic inheritance and deficient education was a fatal blow to her future chances for marriage.[20]

While Jung's thesis earned him a medical degree, its publication humiliated his young cousin, who felt betrayed by the man she had admired and trusted. Ellenberger described the consequences for Hélène and her family and even for Jung:

> The characters in the story were immediately recognized and it aroused a storm of indignation among the Preiswerk family. . . . Carl complained about the "narrow mindedness" of the *Preiswerkerei*. Actually it seemed quite possible that it cost him his career in Basel, so he shifted to Zurich.[21]

In 1903, a year after Jung finished his thesis, Hélène and her sister left Basel for Montpellier, France, where they studied dressmaking. She died, unmarried, of tuberculosis in 1911 at the young age of thirty. Does the gravity of Jung's deceit in this story reside only in the immature failings of a young and ambitious man toward his admiring but naïve cousin? Or might it call into question the validity of the research?

FRANK MILLER

In his article "A Woman Called Frank," Sonu Shamdasani wrote:

> The Mad Miss Miller. . . straightjacketed [sic] in a diagnosis of
> schizophrenia . . . . It is astonishing that Frank Miller, as if buried
> under the landslide of the violent eruption of the text(s), has
> not been studied to date—despite the fact that she provoked
> the longest case study . . . in the collection of Jung's works. Are
> we to view the figure of Frank Miller as an accessory draped
> around the body of the text—a scarf, a stocking, a cape, or a
> lingering perfume—that has not been worthy of serious
> consideration? Have we lost Jung's Ariadne, who guided him
> through the labyrinth?[22]

Frank Miller was born on 11 July 1878, to Frank and Bessie Miller in
Mobile, Alabama, and named after her father.[23] As a young woman, she
traveled throughout Europe, lived in Russia for two years, and studied at
universities in Berlin, Lausanne, and Geneva. At the University of Geneva
she met professor of psychology Théodore Flournoy. While a student there,
she published a manuscript of visions and poetry in 1905 in the *Archives
de Psychologie*.[24] Flournoy, who was something of a mentor for Jung in his
early career, wrote an introduction.[25]

Frank Miller's highly original text is an amalgam of poetry and theory.
The first section, "The Phenomena of Transitory Suggestion or of
Instantaneous Autosuggestion," is followed by a "dream poem," "Glory to
God." A poem entitled "The Moth and the Sun" and a story with a Native
American guide entitled *"Chiwantopei:* A Hypnogogic Drama" precedes
her concluding "Remarks and Explanatory Notes." Her manuscript is the
work of a poet and creative writer and gives evidence that Frank Miller
may have been the first to conceive what Jung later called active imagination.

When she returned to the United States in 1900, she developed her
interest in the customs of other countries into a series of lectures. She
described her experiences in Europe while dressed in national costumes.[26]
Her lectures were well received and the reviews described an " excellent
resumé . . . [of] social, literary, and political conditions," noting that "the
artistic personality of the speaker . . . and the sympathetic quality of her
manner . . . made the lecture unusually pleasing."[27]

In 1909, Frank Miller was briefly admitted to Danvers State Hospital
in Massachusetts. The medical record indicated that "no hallucinations or
delusions" were present and that her "consciousness [was] clear and
apprehension unclouded."[28] She was admitted by Charles Ricksher, a

former research associate of Jung. He gave her a diagnosis of "psychopathy," which, as Bair has pointed out, was a catch-all diagnosis often applied at the turn of the twentieth century to independent or artistic women who chose not to marry.[29] Miller herself expressed frustration about her hospitalization, saying that she had only desired rest and was not hallucinating or under any delusions at the time.[30] One week later Miller was discharged into the care of an aunt. Subsequently, Frank Miller disappeared from the historical record.[31]

Jung used Miller's manuscript as the basis for his *Wandlungen und Symbole der Libido* (1912; published in English in 1916 as *Psychology of the Unconscious*),[32] the volume that finalized his split from Freud. In *Analytical Psychology: Notes on the Seminar Given in 1925*, Jung wrote that the Miller fantasies "acted like a catalyser upon all the material I had gathered together in my mind. I saw in Miss Miller a person who, like myself, had had mythological fantasies, fantasies and dreams of a thoroughly impersonal character."[33] He continued:

> She took over my fantasy and became stage director to it. . . . In other words she became an anima figure, a carrier of an inferior function of which I was very little conscious. . . . Or, to put it even more strongly, passive thinking seemed to me to be such a weak and perverted thing that I could only handle it through a diseased woman.[34]

In the same 1925 lectures, Jung stated that his original diagnosis of "disease," which he had first put forth in 1912, had been affirmed by a letter he received after the war from Miss Miller's doctor in America that stated that she "had become entirely deranged" and had been hospitalized in 1909. While Jung was willing to admit that Frank Miller had been "stage director" to his fantasies, he was unwilling to let her occupy that space permanently. He appropriated her gifts and made them his own, as he reveals in this quote from 1925:

> The material could not fail to make a great impression on me. . . . One of the most important influences was that I elaborated Miss Miller's morbidity into myths in a way satisfactory to myself, and so I assimilated the Miller side of myself, which did me much good. To speak figuratively, I found a lump of clay, turned it into gold and put it in my pocket.[35]

In the German 1925 edition of *Wandlungen und Symbole der Libido,* Jung revealed that he had harbored doubts about whether he "should dare to disclose analytically the private affairs which the authoress . . . had handed over to the general public." He concluded that his "total lack of personal ties with Miss Miller allowed me free speech." Even more remarkably, he convinced himself that because Frank Miller was not his client, he was "absolved . . . from everything one would allow a lady in terms of courtesy which does affect the course of reasoning." In Jung's mind, his motive of contributing to scientific knowledge trumped other considerations: "I wished to demonstrate her individual secret as universally valid. For that reason I took up the task of this analysis for which the authoress perhaps gives me little thanks."[36]

Shamdasani has noted that while many had assumed that the unusual name of "Frank Miller" was a pseudonym, Jung was silent about the issue until the 1924 edition of *Wandlungen und Symbole,* where he claimed for the first time that it *was* a pseudonym as he "raised the curtain on her breakdown."[37] Jung's diagnosis of Frank Miller as a mentally unstable woman may have had serious consequences for his subject, but we cannot know. One must wonder if her anonymity following her release at Danvers State Hospital was not forced upon her by the notoriety that Jung may have created for her. Like Jung himself, she too had encountered the unconscious through what he later called active imagination. Hers was not a medium's encounter with other worlds like Hélène's but a confrontation with images from her own creative unconscious; in other words, the work of a visionary artist and psychic explorer much like Jung himself. As was the case for many before her, she experienced the tragic fate suffered by nontraditional women in the Victorian period, their independence and creative spirits punished, shamed, and even institutionalized.[38] It was not until 1961 that philosopher Gaston Bachelard restored her standing as a poet in *The Flame of a Candle.*[39]

Shamdasani wondered why

> Jung, who had done so much to counter the view of schizophrenia as a disease process, described Frank Miller as "morbid," "diseased," and "deranged.". . . How much do such appellations rightfully belong to her and how much to Jung's mad anima? Did Jung have any ethical qualms about writing his study of a living person whom he had never met and of subsequently revealing her breakdown?[40]

Certainly Jung's 450 pages of amplification of Miss Miller's meager fifteen pages of text combined with his grave diagnosis of a woman he had never met recall disturbing similarities with the case of his young cousin Hélène.

Sabina Spielrein

In 1905, Jung presented two papers on a case of obsessional neurosis, combining Freud's method of psychoanalysis with the word-association experiment. The subject of that paper was nineteen-year-old Sabina Spielrein, a daughter of a wealthy Jewish merchant from Rostov-on-Don in Russia and the oldest of five children. Her younger sister had died in childhood and her relationship with her brothers was strained; they were witnesses to her spankings by her father, and she was humiliated in their presence. Her mother was described as "vain" and her father as "tyrannical."[41] She went to private school in Warsaw and was fluent in seven languages.[42] She had come to Switzerland to enter medical school. Instead, disabled by psychiatric symptoms, she was admitted to the Burghölzli Hospital in 1904.

Jung first described Spielrein to Freud in a letter dated 23 October 1906. "I am currently treating an hysteric with your method. Difficult case, 20-year-old Russian girl student, ill for 6 years."[43] He continued, "First trauma between 3rd and 4th year. Saw her father spanking her brother on the bare bottom. Powerful impression. Couldn't help thinking afterward that she had defecated on her father's hand, from the 4th to 7th year convulsive attempts to defecate on her own feet . . . accompanied by vigorous, blissfully shuddersome feelings. Later this phenomenon was superseded by vigorous masturbation."[44]

But in April 1905, Eugen Bleuler, her chief doctor and head of the Burghölzli clinic, said that she was "not mentally ill" but was merely being treated for "a nervous complaint with hysterical symptoms." Along with Jung, he recommended that she re-enroll in the medical school.[45] She resumed her medical studies that same month and was discharged from the hospital on 1 June 1905. She continued to see Jung informally as an outpatient.

Jung described the complexity of the doctor-patient relationship between himself and Spielrein in 1905 in a report to Freud that was never delivered. There he described her as a "young girl who in the course of her treatment has had the *bad luck to fall in love with me*."[46] Similarly, when Jung received a letter sometime in June 1909 from Sabina's mother, who was concerned about inappropriateness between him and her daughter, he responded that the best protection her daughter had was to make their relationship officially "professional" by paying him as her doctor![47] Revealing more than professional feelings for her, Jung pleaded with Spielrein on 4 December 1908, "Give me back in the moment of my need some of the love and guilt and altruism I was able to give you when you were ill. I'm the one who is ill."[48]

Their relationship remained ambivalent throughout. When Jung began to pull away, Spielrein sought the help of Freud as Jung's respected colleague, and Freud entered the picture as negotiator and confessor to them both. On 11 June 1909, she wrote to Freud seeking his assistance. She described the dynamics of their relationship: "Four and a half years ago, Dr. Jung was my doctor, then he became my friend and finally my 'poet,' i.e. my beloved. Eventually he came to me and things went as they usually do with 'poetry.'"[49] Freud responded by contacting Jung, and together the two men discussed in writing the nature of her anal eroticism and the troubling aspects of transference. Freud declared that "the way these women manage to charm us with every conceivable psychic perfection until they have attained their purpose is one of nature's greatest spectacles."[50] He encouraged Spielrein to "suppress and eradicate" her feelings for Jung.[51]

In January 1911, Sabina took her medical exams and passed with honors. Her father came to Zurich to take her back to Russia. She noted in her diary:

> My friend said in parting that I will write an excellent exam because at present I am in league with the devil. May that be true. My friend and I had the tenderest "poetry" last Wednesday. What will come of that? Make something good of it, Fate, and let me love him nobly.[52]

On 19 January 1911, her journal notes simply, "'He is gone, and 'tis good thus.' Good at least that my parents are now happy. 'Ah, yes, what will happen now?'"[53]

Throughout their relationship, Spielrein talked of a symbolic child she named Siegfried that would be born of their love. Jung feared that Sabina longed for a real child, but when she sent him her medical thesis in 1911, she wrote in her cover letter to him, "Receive now the product of our love, the project which is your little son Siegfried."[54] Spielrein concluded her analytical work with Jung in 1912.

While "Siegfried" served as the symbol for Sabina's creativity, Jung had a quite different experience of the same image several years after she completed her thesis. In December 1913, he dreamed:

> I was with an unknown, brown skinned man, a savage, in a lonely rocky mountain landscape. . . . Then I heard Siegfried's horn sounding over the mountains and I knew we had to kill him. . . . [He approached on] a chariot of bones, he drove at a

furious speed, we shot at him and he plunged down struck dead. Filled with disgust and remorse for having destroyed something so great and beautiful, I turned to flee. . . . Rain began to fall, and I knew it would wipe out all traces of the dead. *I had escaped the danger of discovery; life would go on, but an unbearable feeling of guilt remained.*[55]

What was the cause of Jung's guilt? Did the love affair with Spielrein prefigure his dissolution the following year, in the period that has come to be known as his encounter with the unconscious? Might Jung's grief over its loss suggest deeper, more likely causes for his unraveling than his break with Freud over philosophical differences?

Jung revealed the depth of his feelings about the affair in his last letter to Spielrein, dated 1 September 1919. He wrote it in the third person:

The love of S for J made the latter aware of something he had previously only vaguely suspected, that is of a power in the unconscious that shapes one's destiny, a power which later led him to things of the greatest importance. The relationship had to be "sublimated" because otherwise it would have led him to delusion and madness (the concretization of the unconscious). Occasionally one must be unworthy, simply in order to be able to go on living.[56]

Unlike Hélène Preiswerk and Frank Miller, Sabina Spielrein's post-Jung life included an analytical career. Her dissertation on a case of schizophrenia made a significant contribution to the field. Her first article, "Destruction as the Cause of Coming into Being" (1912),[57] anticipated Freud's ideas about the death instinct in *Beyond the Pleasure Principle* (1920) by almost ten years. She published many other psychoanalytic papers in French and German.[58]

Yet her name is not known as one of the pioneers of her field. Sabina Spielrein's history was almost completely excised due to her controversial relationships with the two titans of psychoanalysis. Psychoanalyst Johannes Cremerius noted this in the mid-1980s: "We are left with the question of why an analyst who was so distinguished in the early years of psychoanalysis is not well known, why her papers are not cited? They are truly 'forgotten.'"[59] Cremerius described Sabina's "terrible story . . . [as] demonstrat[ing] the complicity of two men against the woman who had allowed herself to be seduced by one of them."[60] Certainly Sabina fell into the shadow of the conflict between Jung and Freud, and to speak her name recalled for each their own human shortcomings and failures. Little did she realize that her love and affection for them would forever encapsulate her in their silence.

ANTONIA WOLFF

Writing to Freud in advance of the Weimar conference in 1911, Jung introduced Antonia Wolff "as his new discovery" and praised her for her "excellent feeling for religion and philosophy."[61] In 1910, nineteen-year-old Toni had been brought to Jung by her mother for treatment of her depression following the sudden death of her father. According to Barbara Hannah, Jung saw Toni analytically for about three years, but not after that. After her analysis ended, Toni fell back into a depression. Jung "hesitated . . . for he knew how drawn he was to her and he was most reluctant to inflict any suffering on his wife and family."[62] Eventually she became his secretary and began working closely with him in that capacity.

In 1914, two weeks after Emma Jung gave birth to a daughter, Jung and Toni Wolff took a vacation in Ravenna, "leaving Emma and the baby to be cared for by her mother, and the older children by his."[63] Jung told Emma that he could never accord Toni a status less than "his other wife."[64] Bair records that "'Toni was always there,'" at all the Jung events and in the midst of the Jung family, even at the Sunday luncheons that had previously "been sacrosanct family occasions." At lectures, "C. G., Emma and Toni would arrive and depart together [while] the two women would be seated in [equally valued] positions" in the lecture hall."[65] When Jung became interested in alchemy in the mid-1920s, Toni began to differ with him over the direction of Jungian psychology. She wanted him to pay more attention to current psychological research than to alchemy. Jung experienced her disinterest in alchemy as a personal betrayal, telling Harry Murray, "'All of a sudden Toni Wolff went out of my life just as fast as she came in it. All of a sudden, that was the end.'"[66] Well-known analyst Maria Louise von Franz also commented on Wolff's changing role with Jung:

> I knew about [Jung's relationship with] Toni Wolff almost at once. . . . [Toni's] big mistake was in not being enthusiastic about alchemy. It was unfortunate that she refused to follow him there, because otherwise he would not have thrown her over to collaborate with me. He would have used me just for translating, and he would have confided in her. But she wasn't interested. She was too much a slightly conventional Christian, and she refused to follow him.[67]

Toni died on 21 March 1953, at age sixty-five. Only Emma attended the funeral. On Easter that year, several weeks after Toni's death, Jung dreamed of Toni dressed in a gown of many colors, predominately royal blue, like a kingfisher's. He felt comforted by the dream.[68] In her memory he carved Chinese characters into a stone that said, "Toni Wolff. Lotus. Nun. Mysterious."[69] It resides in the garden of his Küsnacht home. One wonders if the figure Jung carved on the outer wall at Bollingen after Emma's death, which he described as "obviously my anima in the guise of a millennia-old ancestress," evoked the spirit of Toni. Similarly, might the nearby carving Jung identified as "the Russian bear which starts things rolling" be an allusion to Sabina Spielrein?[70] If these, in fact, are their memorials, they are as private as Jung's grief and as mysterious as the lives of all four of these women, each lost as the objects of Jung's projections, subsumed as the proofs to his theories, encased in his secret guilt and personal failings.

NOTES

[1] Mana is an anthropological term referring to the divinely inspired or supernatural powers that are believed to belong to important leaders such as kings, tribal elders, or shamans. Its modern-day equivalent would be charisma or personal magnetism.

[2] Susan Rowland, *Jung: A Feminist Revision* (Cambridge: Polity, 2002), pp. 15–16.

[3] *Ibid.,* p. 19.

[4] James Hillman, "Some Early Background to Jung's Ideas: Notes on C. G. Jung's Medium by Stefanie Zumstein Preiswerk," in *Spring: An Annual of Archetypal Psychology and Thought* (New York: Spring Publications, 1976), p. 131.

[5] Christine Marks, "Hysteria, Doctor-Patient Relationships, and Identity Boundaries in Siri Hustvedt's *What I Loved,*" *Gender Forum: An Internet Journal for Gender Studies* 25 (2009): 2, available at http://www.genderforum.org/issues/literature-and-medicine-i/hysteria-doctor-patient-relationships-and-identity-boundaries-in-siri-hustvedts-what-i-loved/?0=.

[6] Jung, "Individual Dream Symbolism in Relation to Alchemy" (1936), in *The Collected Works of C. G. Jung,* vol. 12, *Psychology and Alchemy,* ed. and trans. Gerhard Adler and R. F. C. Hull (Princeton, N.J.: Princeton University Press, 1968), §219.

[7] Jung, "The Symbolism of the Mandala" (1953), in *Psychology and Alchemy,* §219. Jung's parentheses.

[8] Judith Butler, *Precarious Life: The Powers of Mourning and Violence* (London, New York: Verso, 2004), pp. xvii–xviii.

⁹ Jung, "On the Psychology and Pathology of So-Called Occult Phenomena" (1957), in *The Collected Works of C. G. Jung,* vol. 1, *Psychiatric Studies,* ed. and trans. Gerhard Adler and R. F. C. Hull (Princeton, N.J.: Princeton University Press, 1970), §36.

¹⁰ *Ibid.*

¹¹ William B. Goodheart, "C. G. Jung's First Patient: On the Seminal Emergence of Jung's Thought," *Journal of Analytical Psychology* 29, no. 1 (1984): 1–34.

¹² Jung, "On the Psychology of the Unconscious" (1953), in *The Collected Works of C. G. Jung,* vol. 7, *Two Essays in Analytical Psychology,* ed. and trans. Gerhard Adler and R. F. C. Hull (Princeton, N.J.: Princeton University Press, 1967), §199. My italics.

¹³ Goodheart, "C. G. Jung's First Patient," p. 1.

¹⁴ Rowland, *Jung: A Feminist Revision*, pp. 5–6ff.

¹⁵ *Ibid.,* p. 43.

¹⁶ Gerhard Wehr, *An Illustrated Biography of C. G. Jung,* trans. Michael H. Kohn (Boston: Shambala, 1989), p. 50.

¹⁷ Deirdre Bair, *Jung: A Biography* (Boston: Little, Brown & Company, 2003), p. 48.

¹⁸ *Ibid.,* pp. 48–49.

¹⁹ Jung, "On the Psychology of So-Called Occult Phenomena," §§37–38.

²⁰ John Kerr, *A Most Dangerous Method: The Story of Jung, Freud, and Sabina Spielrein* (New York: Alfred A. Knopf, 1993), pp. 54–56.

²¹ H. F. Ellenberger, "The Story of Helene Preiswerk: A Critical Study with New Documents," *History of Psychiatry* 2, no. 5 (1991): 51.

²² Sonu Shamdasani, "A Woman Called Frank," *Spring: An Annual of Archetypal Psychology and Jungian Thought* 50 (1990): 26–27.

²³ *Ibid.,* p. 31.

²⁴ *Ibid.,* p. 42. Although Miller wrote her text in English, it was first published in French as "Quelques faits d'imagination créatrice subconsciente," *Archives de psychologie* (Geneva) 5 (1906). James H. Hyslop retranslated it back into English one year later, published as "Some Instances of Subconscious Creative Imagination," *Journal of the American Society for Psychical Research* 1, no. 6 (1907). See Bair, *Jung,* 718n65.

²⁵ Flournoy's study of a medium he called Hélène Smith had strongly influenced Jung's theories about the psychic abilities of Hélène Preiswerk. Flournoy's study of Smith was entitled *From India to Planet Mars: A Study of a Case of Somnambulism with Glossolalia* (1899; repr., New York: Harper and Bros., 1900). For Jung's embrace of Flournoy's theories, see F. X.

Charet, *Spiritualism and the Foundations of C. G. Jung's Psychology* (Albany, N.Y.: SUNY Press, 1993), p. 232; Sonu Shamdasani's "Introduction" to *From India to the Planet Mars, a Study of a Case of Somnambulism with Glossolalia* (Princeton, N.J.: Princeton University Press, 1994); and Sonu Shamdasani, *Jung and the Making of Modern Psychology: The Dream of a Science* (Cambridge, Cambridge University Press, 2003).

[26] Shamdasani, "A Woman Called Frank," pp. 33–34.

[27] *Columbia Spectator,* 3 December 1901, p. 7, quoted in Shamdasani, "A Woman Called Frank," p. 34.

[28] Shamdasani, "A Woman Called Frank," pp. 31–32.

[29] Bair, *Jung,* p. 213.

[30] Shamdasani, " A Woman Called Frank," pp. 30–32.

[31] *Ibid.*

[32] C. G. Jung, *Wandlungen und Symbole der Libido: Beitrage zur Entwicklungsgeschichte des Denkens* (Leipzig: Deuticke, 1912); first translated into English as C. G. Jung, *Psychology of the Unconscious: A Study of the Transformations and Symbolisms of the Libido,* trans. Beatrice Moses Hinkle (New York: Moffat, Yard, and Co., 1916).

[33] C. G. Jung, *Analytical Psychology: Notes on the Seminar Given in 1925,* ed. William McGuire (Princeton, N.J.: Princeton University Press, 1989), p. 24.

[34] *Ibid.,* pp. 27–28.

[35] Jung, *Analytical Psychology: Notes on the Seminar Given in 1925,* p. 31.

[36] C. G. Jung, *Wandlungen und Symbole der Libido* (Deuticke, 1925), trans. Michael Münchow in Shamdasani, "A Woman Called Frank," p. 29. This copy was omitted from subsequent versions of the text.

[37] Shamdasani, "A Woman Called Frank," pp. 30–31. The revelation is in C. G. Jung, *Symbols of Transformation,* vol. 5 of *The Collected Works of C. G. Jung,* edited and translated by G. Adler and R. F. C. Hull (Princeton, N.J.: Princeton University Press, 1967), p. xxviii. Shamdasani notes that Miller's name was revealed as a pseudonym in two other places in the *Collected Works (ibid.,* §46 and p. 485), but in both instances the information was inserted by William McGuire. He cites a letter from McGuire to the Editors of *The Collected Works,* 29 November 1956, Bollingen Collection, Library of Congress.

[38] Bair, *Jung,* p. 214.

[39] Shamdasani, "A Woman Called Frank," p. 49.

[40] *Ibid.,* pp. 28–29.

[41] Bair, *Jung,* p. 87.

⁴² *Ibid.*

⁴³ William McGuire, ed., *The Freud/Jung Letters*, Bollingen Series XCIV (Princeton, N.J.: Princeton University Press, 1974), p. 7.

⁴⁴ *Ibid.*

⁴⁵ Medical certificate signed by Eugen Bleuler, 27 April 1905, in "Burghölzli Hospital Records of Sabina Spielrein," trans. Dorothee Steffens, revised by Barbara Wharton, *Journal of Analytical Psychology* 46, no. 1 (2001): 35.

⁴⁶ Jung to Freud, 25 September 1905, quoted in Zvi Lothane, "Tender Love and Transference: Unpublished Letters of C. G. Jung and Sabina Spielrein," in *Sabina Spielrein: Forgotten Pioneer of Psychoanalysis,* ed. Coline Covington and Barbara Wharton (East Sussex: Brunner Routledge, 2003), p. 196, Lothane's italics.

⁴⁷ See Aldo Carotenuto, *A Secret Symmetry: Sabina Spielrein between Jung and Freud* (London: Routledge & Kegan Paul, 1980), p. 94.

⁴⁸ Jung quoted in "The Letters of C. G. Jung to Sabina Spielrein," trans. Barbara Wharton, in Covington and Wharton, *Sabina Spielrein,* p. 38.

⁴⁹ Kerr, *A Most Dangerous Method,* p. 223.

⁵⁰ *Ibid.,* p. 219.

⁵¹ *Ibid.,* p. 220.

⁵² *Ibid.,* p. 313.

⁵³ *Ibid.*

⁵⁴ *Ibid.,* p. 324.

⁵⁵ C. G. Jung, *Memories, Dreams, Reflections,* ed. Aniela Jaffé (London: Collins and Routledge & Kegan Paul, 1963), p. 173, my italics.

⁵⁶ Jung quoted in Carotenuto, *A Secret Symmetry,* p. 190; Carotenuto quoted in Kerr, *A Most Dangerous Method,* p. 491, Jung's parentheses.

⁵⁷ "Die Destruktion als Ursache des Werdens," *Jahrbuch für psychoanalytische und psychopathologische Forschungen* 4 (1912): 465–503; translated into English as "Destruction as the Cause of Coming into Being," *Journal of Analytical Psychology* 39, no. 2 (1994): 155–186.

⁵⁸ Johannes Cremerius, "Foreword to Aldo Carotenuto's *Tagebuch einer heimlichen Symmetrie*" (1986), in Covington and Wharton, *Sabina Spielrein,* p. 70.

⁵⁹ *Ibid.*

⁶⁰ *Ibid.,* p. 63.

⁶¹ Bair, *Jung,* p. 200.

⁶² Barbara Hannah, *Jung: His Life and Work. A Biographical Memoir* (1997; repr., Wilmette, Ill.: Chiron Publications, 1999), p. 119.

⁶³ Bair, *Jung,* p. 248.

⁶⁴ *Ibid.,* p. 266.

⁶⁵ *Ibid.,* p. 265.

⁶⁶ *Ibid.,* p. 390.

⁶⁷ *Ibid.,* p. 371, Bair's brackets around "Jung's relationship with."

⁶⁸ *Ibid.,* p. 559.

⁶⁹ *Ibid.*

⁷⁰ C. G. Jung and Aniela Jaffé, *C. G. Jung: Word and Image,* vol. 2, Bollingen Series XCVII (Princeton, N.J.: Princeton University Press, 1979), p. 194.

9

The Meaning of Conflict in Couples: A Jungian Approach to Couples Therapy

Christian Roesler

I think one of the problems in marriage is that people don't realize what it is. They think it is a long love affair and it isn't. Marriage has nothing to do with being happy. It has to do with being transformed, and when the transformation is realized it is a magnificent experience. But you have to submit. You have to yield. You have to give. You can't just dictate.

—Joseph Campbell[1]

INTRODUCTION

The motivation to contribute to a Jungian approach to couples therapy stems from my experience in two different fields: I am a Jungian analyst, and I have worked with couples intensively for over fifteen years. Although Jung did not provide a model of couples therapy per se, he left a legacy that others have built upon. Like Polly Young-Eisendrath and James Hollis, for instance, I have come to realize that analytical psychology offers a unique resource for a profound understanding of relationships and their dynamics.[2]

FUNDAMENTAL PRINCIPLES

Before proceeding to focus on a Jungian approach to couples therapy, it is helpful to review some basic guiding principles.

- In Jung's analytical psychology the unconscious is understood, in part, as a source of unrealized potential, meaning, and guidance for the individual's search for wholeness (individuation). In other words, Jungian psychology views the unconscious as a positive, constructive force that drives the individual toward his or her full potential. As a whole, this process is referred to as "individuation."

• The individuation process shows itself in symbols and images; that is, in creative impulses that are symbolized in dreams, fantasies, and creative work—and also in neurotic symptoms and conflicts.

• The psyche is organized in polarities or pairs of opposites. A bias toward one pole tends to be compensated for by its counterforce. The individuation process and psychic life in general is thus based on tensions between antagonistic forces and on compensating for the imbalances that arise from them. The unconscious with its constructive orientation toward wholeness strives to compensate—that is, to bring certain imbalances in the psyche into equilibrium.

• Psychotherapy in this context entails using the constructive and compensatory impulses of the unconscious to support individuation by integrating them into the conscious mind.

• An active understanding of the unconscious requires an interpretation of the symbols it offers to us.

• In Jungian psychology the idea of the unconscious is further expanded in the concept of the "collective unconscious"; that is, a field of unconsciousness in which all of humanity participates and to which all members contribute. This "interactive field," as Nathan Schwartz-Salant has more recently called it, can function as a vessel of unconscious communication between two or more people.[3]

THE IMPORTANCE OF RELATIONSHIP FOR INDIVIDUATION

If a general reading of Jung leaves some of us with the impression that individuation has little to do with outer relationships, we can recall the value that Jung attributes to the analytical pair—patient and psychotherapist—as significant and mutual carriers of the process. In fact, Jung more universally stresses that "the conscious achievement of inner unity [i.e., individuation] clings to human relationships as to an indispensable condition, for without the conscious acknowledgement and acceptance of our fellowship with those around us there can be no synthesis of the personality."[4]

In other words, according to Jung, we need relationship, and learning to relate is part and parcel of the individuation journey itself: "Individuation has two principal aspects: in the first place it is an internal and subjective process of integration, and in the second it is an equally indispensable process of objective relationship. Neither can exist without the other."[5] Jung's writings are rich with observations of the dynamics of relationships, such as those between parent and child[6] and, indeed, between marital partners.[7] Not to be overlooked is Jung's extensive work on the impact of psychological type in relationships,[8] a concept that encompasses the idea of archetypal opposition and has been applied in marriage counseling, among other ways.[9] Indeed, very early in his work Jung reveals a systemic understanding of relationships within the family, although he did not actually term it as such.

BEYOND FUNCTIONING WELL

The epigraph by Joseph Campbell that began this chapter concisely expresses a basic assumption that informs my work. He postulates that the majority of couples mistakenly believe that close relationships are predestined to lead to happiness. Like Campbell, I regard relationship primarily as a "place" in which the transformation of one's personality as well as the transformation of the couple itself can be initiated and fostered. Rather than always evoking happiness and harmony, this process is experienced as conflicted and sometimes painful. The approach I present here explores the deeper meanings in the inevitable conflicts that couples endure.

In analytical psychology we understand psychological development from the perspective of the Self; that is, the Self initiates and shapes the course of individuation. Here, the Self is understood as unconscious knowledge of the intrinsic uniqueness—the true being of the person—and at the same time as the potential wholeness of the personality, including the shadow aspects.

In the lives of couples, Self- and individuation impulses are especially manifest during unavoidable episodes and periods of conflict. An intimate relationship is unique in that nowhere else do we share our deepest feelings with a partner and in so doing expose ourselves at great depth. In close relationships we become inevitably confronted with shadows, both our own and those of our partners.

During the course of long-term and close relationships, both partners are confronted with one another's qualities and weaknesses, and both must find ways to deal with the weaknesses in particular. Indeed, we experience our inner Self most profoundly through intimate relations with another being. This implies that we ought to reconsider the notion that all conflicted relationships are flawed and instead recognize in such relationships fertile soil for individuation. This idea can be found not only in Jung but also in the *Begegnungsphilosophie,* or the philosophy of encounter, of Ludwig Feuerbach, of Ludwig Binswanger, and of Martin Buber, for whom "I" can only grow in relation with "you."[10]

Jungian analyst Adolf Guggenbühl-Craig articulates similar ideas in his book on marriage.[11] He argues that marriage or long-term relationships can support and advance individuation for both partners like nothing else. In such a relationship, each partner can serve as a mirror of the other's innermost reality. However, Guggenbühl makes very clear that not all relationships are suited or destined to withstand the "marriage of individuation." Such a union requires both partners' willingness to open themselves to Self-encounter, to endure the conflict and pain that arises from this as well as from confrontation with the shadow and unconscious, and, finally, to find ground for constructive change in the experience.

Unconscious Choice of Partner: Where Individuation Begins

The fact that we choose one particular person out of many for a long-term relationship makes much sense from the standpoint of depth psychology. We assume that the unconscious plays a key role, for it leads us to choose partners with whom we experience conflict exactly around those points at which our own psychological problems remain unresolved.

This means that the conflicts we experience with our partners are actually appeals to face our own issues. Our partner is our closest "other," the person with whom we share our deepest emotions. Thus, he or she can reveal our weaknesses, which can be quite hurtful sometimes and, of course, can bring about conflict. The fact that we constantly reenter the same quarrels and reproaches need not mean that we require fixing or that we must learn proper communication skills or that we must break up the relationship. Instead, we can embrace conflict as fuel for the individuation process, as David Hewison reminds us:

> The "gathering of the world" cannot take place in isolation as it
> is driven not just by archetypal potentialities in the person, but
> is also dependent on the experiences available to them and in

particular, the experience of intimate relationships in which there
is the opportunity for a process of immersion, withdrawal and
re-immersion in a shared, meaningful, psychological life. Adult
couple relationships are therefore one of the key areas of
emotional life for the individuation process.[12]

But what is it that might be achieved through conflict in couples? For Jung
the meaning of human life is the development toward a state of (greater)
wholeness. Wholeness in Jungian terminology does not mean "proper
functioning" but rather movement toward our full potential and possibilities
and, further, our coming to terms with the rejected parts of our partners
and selves. This is why the process of individuation is often rather hurtful
and is inescapably associated with conflict. However, it is in this very
development toward wholeness that we can discover the persons we are
meant to be and thus find greater fulfillment in our lives.

Our psyche chooses a particular partner because it seems to
instinctively know that this person can help us get in touch with the rejected
and unconscious parts of our personality. It is especially in such intimate,
long-term relationship that the deepest emotions and conflicts come to the
surface of our souls. We could also say that this is the reason that so many
people invest such great energy in searching for a life partner. In fact, the
search for a partner includes a search for one's own wholeness.

POLARIZATION OF OPPOSITES

Jung conceived the psyche as being constituted of opposing forces. The
tension and antagonism between these forces creates vital life energy. In
the long run, our psyche strives to reach a state of wholeness or, we could
say, an ongoing compensation of antagonistic forces. In other words, the
psyche strives to encompass all of life's opposites. We call it "polarization,"
however, when the opposites are driven apart, with the effect that they
clash or become isolated or one rules over the other.

In my work as a couples therapist, I often observe the dynamic of
polarization. Typically, the two consulting partners are on bad terms with
one another; each blames the other for intolerable peculiarities and deficits.
When we take a closer look at the criticisms, it is evident that the two
have taken up extremely opposing positions around a common core. When
this happens, the couple has entered a shared field of polarized opposites.

Such polarization usually takes years to unfold and tends to stem from
attitudes or qualities that can become one-sided personality traits. Indeed,
these traits emerge as fundamental pairs of opposites that affect psychic

life and underlie the psyche's striving for equilibrium. The following list, while certainly not complete, provides an overview of such traits:

intimacy versus distance	introversion versus extroversion
devotion versus rejection	activity versus passivity
commitment versus autonomy	change versus consistency
dependence versus independence	irrationality versus rationality
weakness versus strength	emotion versus reason
submission versus dominance (power)	letting go versus controlling
grandiosity versus inferiority	acceptance versus confrontation
communality versus obstinacy	cooperation versus competition

Because it is often the case that people unconsciously choose partners because of shared complexes, in long-term relationships these complexes lead each partner to habitually assume a characteristic position in areas of conflict. The effect is that the two approach conflict with attitudes that add up to pair of polar opposites. In other words, each member of couple unconsciously chooses a partner who compensates for unconscious and unsolved problems. Indeed, at the beginning of a relationship it is often precisely the compensatory qualities of the partner that fascinate and attract. But when we ask partners in couples therapy what initially drew them toward each other, they often state that those initially fascinating traits are exactly the things that so irritate them now.

Close examination reveals a vague, mostly unconscious fantasy that the solution for one's own problems lies in the bond with the other person, or at least that because of the relationship, the problems will not be so predominant. From the perspective of the Self, the deeper meaning of the relationship is that the chosen partner will inevitably confront the individual with the very problems that at some level he or she hoped to avoid. The process of polarization usually occurs in long-term couple relationships and takes years to unfold. From the beginning, each partner is biased toward one of the poles. Eventually, over time, the partners each gravitate toward a less-balanced position on the issue at hand.

Some models of couples therapy have a rather negative opinion of polarization, tending to treat it as a deficit and sign of pathology.[13] In contrast, Jung allows us to frame polarization within the context of projection and to see both dynamics as part of the process that leads to the possibility of individuation.

A POSITIVE VIEW OF PROJECTION

Projection is the act of attributing exclusively to others features that dwell as unconscious potentials within ourselves. Projected contents may amount to attractive qualities or to annoying, even repulsive, characteristics. Either way, a first step toward conflict resolution as well as toward self-realization is to recognize projection for what it is. A further step is to actively "take back" and integrate our projections, which means to become conscious of the projected content, to come to terms with it within ourselves, and to perhaps bring it to fruition in our outer lives. Thus, in a Jungian perspective, projection is *valued*—for it makes visible in the "other" Self-contents that would otherwise remain rejected by or unconscious to the perceiving "I."

Here I want to emphasize the aspect of mutuality in couples, whereby both partners simultaneously project onto the other. The projected traits or features that belong to both partners constitute common unconscious themes. While involved in the projective dynamic, each partner lives out his or her particular bias, thereby unconsciously compensating for the other's position. In long-term relationships, it is this sustained, mutually unconscious projection and complementarity that leads to heightened polarization. Yet the same state of affairs provides the energy and seeds for mutual growth, in that both partners are presented with the opportunity to come to terms with their commonly held unconscious themes.

THE SHARED UNCONSCIOUS

How, exactly, does this process of projection work? How can partners delegate and thereby "cause" each other to enact attitudes that could otherwise be lived in their own respective realities? Whereas we have already noted the couple's mutual participation in a field of polarized opposites, I would more generally note their co-creation of and mutual participation in a *common unconscious*. Jung described a similar bond between psychotherapist and patient that "rest[s] on mutual unconsciousness."[14] Jung's remarkable conclusion in a letter to James Kirsch expressed his awareness that all relationships contain this dimension: "In the deepest sense we do not dream from ourselves, but from the space between ourselves and the other."[15] In the common unconscious, in that "space in between," we recognize also Nathan Schwartz-Salant's "interactive field."[16] These are all attempts to localize the invisible but tangible place where partners unconsciously exchange messages and transfer parts of their personalities to one another.

Those of us who work analytically are familiar with the phenomenon. An example would be when we arrive at new insights about our clients' issues in the closed and confidential setting of supervision, and then, before we have the chance to say a single word in a session with the clients based on our new understanding of the case, the clients themselves mention change regarding the same topics.

Jungian psychotherapy entails, among other things, the task of developing ego awareness of the unconscious and its deeper, hidden meanings. The intimacy and emotional intensity of a relationship is especially likely to activate the unconscious and its rich imagery. Whereas in individual therapy these images tend to initially become tangible only through projection onto the therapist, in couples therapy the partners can learn to access the images by seeing them in projection upon one another. Thus, couples have an advantage in their potential to mutually foster the therapeutic process by supporting one another's work with images and with the unconscious in general.

WHY COUPLES DEVELOP A COMMON UNCONSCIOUS

We are more than two ones who, in fusing to become One, remain
only two; we are two ones who have also become a third.
                                                    —James Hollis[17]

Jungian author James Hollis (1998) calls the unconscious fantasy that the solution for our own problems lies in becoming one with the partner the "Eden project."[18] The same basic idea can be found in psychoanalytically oriented couples therapist Jürg Willi's concept of collusion.[19] Couples therapists at London's Tavistock Institute of Marital Studies—who also employ a psychoanalytic approach—have developed a corresponding concept in the "shared unconscious phantasy."[20]

Psychoanalytically oriented practitioners see in the couple's unconscious fantasy and desire for fusion an underlying, shared defense against the fear of loneliness and change. The view of pathology that we detect here becomes more evident in the conception of the shared fantasy as a defensive construct that aims to preserve stability over and against further development:

> When we see a turning away from change and development by the couple, we think not so much of individuals each with powerful narcissistic defences operating separately but simultaneously, but more of an unconscious "agreement" between the couple to stifle growth, for whatever reason. We focus on a shared interaction between them at an unconscious level: each one acts upon and relies upon the other to

maintain a "shared couple defence" against a dangerous and frightening "shared unconscious phantasy" about what development might mean.[21]

A Jungian perspective encompasses but also goes beyond the notion of pathology. In other words, Jung's constructive view allows us to discern healthy motives in the couple's creation of a common unconscious. In fact Jung's genuine—and in my opinion revolutionary—contribution lies in his recognition that the seemingly pathological often evolves into a natural process directed by the Self that seeks the goal of psychological wholeness. This idea is not completely new, since Jung drew upon Plato's philosophy. In his *Symposium*, Plato refers to a myth in which humans originally were orb-like creatures who had been divided into male and female halves. These two halves are searching for each other during their whole life, striving to reunite and regain their native wholeness.[22] The human longing for a couple relationship would then actually be the search for one's own wholeness.

THE COMMON UNCONSCIOUS SYMBOLIZED IN THE *ROSARIUM PHILOSOPHORUM*

Jung translated and employed alchemical imagery, that of the *Rosarium philosophorum* in particular, to symbolize stages of the individuation process, which he understood to unfold mutually, among other places, within analytical relationships. Schwartz-Salant, too, uses the *Rosarium* to illustrate the interactive field, which I regard as the most elaborated concept to date for describing the shared unconscious and the transformation it may contain.[23] The *Rosarium* describes the process of two entities or persons becoming one and separating again. This process gives rise to a third, shared entity. The couple relationship can be understood as a "united duality," a state in which both beings are neither separate nor fused in a negative sense. The great paradox the *Rosarium* describes is the unification of the two basic human needs: to become one with another being and to maintain one's identity as an autonomous individual. This is what the human being seeks in a couple relationship.

Jung himself saw this process in two ways: as the mystical marriage with one's own psyche, as in inner experience (individual wholeness); and as the ability to truly recognize the nature of the other human being, without any projections, in order to enter a real relationship. He stressed that in the final unity a separateness remains; what is important is the process of moving toward wholeness.[24]

Therapeutic Methods and Approaches

The foregoing ideas might be put into practice in couples therapy in a number of ways. An important difference from individual therapy is that the therapist bears direct witness to the couples' mutual strategy of projection and blame, their statements that "if he/she would just change, our problems would be solved." Such polarization can serve as a shared pathological defense against development. Therefore it is crucial in couples therapy to help partners grasp that their conflicts can best be understood as shared, something to which both contribute.

A Jungian approach to couples therapy would raise the question of which archetypes underlie the partners' behavior and lead to their unconscious acting out. In introducing the archetypes we enlist a consciousness-raising device, and we also hope to enlighten the universal and fundamentally human nature of a couple's relationship concerns.[25]

Naturally we confront couples in therapy with their unresolved issues and mutual contributions to conflict. More than this, we open the possibility to discover meaning in conflict, which itself challenges each partner to develop, to grow, to individuate. It can be helpful to point out that the direction of development for each may be visible in the respectively projected traits. It is further helpful to encourage awareness of the complementarity of reproaches. In other words, we support the partners in the realization of the need for each to focus on their own weaknesses and blind spots.

We can explain that conflict in couples makes sense from the perspective of the Self and the unconscious, which arranged their pairing a meaningful way, ultimately with the aim of promoting growth and individuation. We can also show couples the value of surrendering the "Eden project," of giving up the attempt to resolve individual issues by melding together and developing the will to work alone to reclaim and integrate projected parts. I call this process "the inner divorce."

Often both partners feel that actual separation or divorce is the only solution. We try to reframe the situation. While we understand that they want to leave their painful situation behind, we discourage separation, for a breakup does not necessarily bring an inner resolution to their problems. Indeed, a breakup might mean that both would take their unresolved conflicts into the next relationship. The tendency to do so might explain the high rate of divorce in second marriages. However, the point is not to judge whether separation is a solution or not but to encourage an improvement of the presented conditions. Research shows that the majority of couples can resolve their issues when therapeutic support is obtained before all is lost.[26] Of course the result is always open and must be so. The partners make the decisions, and sometimes one or both chooses separation.

Traditional Jungian methods of excavating the unconscious and its archetypal dimensions prove to be very effective, especially as they have been adapted for couples. What I have in mind here are creative approaches of the kind that Jung so encouraged:

The couple can be invited to paint together, to fill a large sheet of paper with color.[27] The resulting picture can be seen to reveal each partner's occupation of psychological space within the relationship as a whole.

In sandplay, couples may be asked to create scenes of their relationship as it appears to them at the moment—and how they would like it to look in the future.[28] It sometimes happens that the scene lacks a figure that symbolizes one of the partners; one approach in such cases is to invite the "missing" partner to fill the gap with his/her chosen figure.[29]

Mutual exploration of dreams also proves to be fruitful. The male partner of a couple that was in therapy with me once dreamed that a lizard and a bird were pressed into a glass bottle; because of the narrow space they started to fight with each other. When asked what the dream meant to him, the man replied, "It is obvious that you cannot put two such different animals into such a tiny space." Based on this I encouraged the husband to speak to his wife in the session about his experience of space in the relationship and his need for more autonomy, which was the first time in his life he had ever done that.

CONCLUSION

In conclusion, a Jungian approach to couples therapy entails the same goals that are contained in Jungian therapy with individuals: We aim to bring the unconscious to light, to support conscious reflection on the contents, and to integrate the perspectives and solutions that the unconscious offers in its symbols.

NOTES

[1] Joseph Campbell, *This Business of the Gods: In Conversation with Fraser Boa* (Caledon, East Ontario: Windrose Publications, 1989), p. 78.

² See Polly Young-Eisendrath, *You're Not What I Expected: Learning to Love the Opposite Sex* (New York: William Morrow & Co., 1993); and James Hollis, *The Eden Project: In Search of the Magical Other* (Toronto: Inner City Books, 1998).

³ Nathan Schwartz-Salant, "On the Interactive Field as the Analytic Object," in *The Interactive Field in Analysis,* ed. Murray Stein (Wilmette, Ill.: Chiron Publications, 1995), pp. 1–36.

⁴ C. G. Jung, "The Psychology of the Transference" (1946), in *The Practice of Psychotherapy,* vol. 16 of *The Collected Works of C.G. Jung,* trans. R. F. C. Hull (Princeton, N.J.: Princeton University Press, 1985), §444.

⁵ *Ibid.,* §448.

⁶ See various chapters on child psychology in C. G. Jung, *The Development of Personality,* vol. 17 of *The Collected Works of C. G. Jung,* ed. and trans. G. Adler and R. F. C. Hull (Princeton, N.J.: Princeton University Press, 1981).

⁷ C. G. Jung, "Marriage as a Psychological Relationship" (1925), in Jung, *Development of Personality,* §§324–345.

⁸ C. G. Jung, *Psychological Types* (1921), vol. 6 of *The Collected Works of C. G. Jung,* ed. and trans. G. Adler and R. F. C. Hull (Princeton, N.J.: Princeton University Press, 1971).

⁹ See for instance Rae Carlson, "Studies of Jungian Typology: III. Personality and Marriage," *Journal of Personality Assessment* 48, no. 1 (1984): 87–94.

¹⁰ See J. Willi, *Ko-Evolution. Die Kunst gemeinsamen Wachsens* (Reinbek: Rowohlt, 1985).

¹¹ Adolf Guggenbühl-Craig, *Marriage: Dead or Alive,* trans. Murray Stein, new ed. (Woodstock, Conn.: Spring Publications, 2001).

¹² David Hewison, "'Oh Rose, Thou Art Sick!' Anti-Individuation Forces in the Film *American Beauty,*" *Journal of Analytical Psychology* 48, no. 5 (2003): 683–704.

¹³ See for instance Jürg Willi, *Couples in Collusion,* trans. Walia Inayat-Khan and Mariusz Tchorek (New York: Jason Aronson, Inc., 1982).

¹⁴ Jung, "The Psychology of Transference," §367.

¹⁵ C. G. Jung to James Kirsch, 29 September 1934, in *Briefe 1906–1961,* ed. Aniela Jaffé (Olten: Walter-Verlag, 1980/81), 3:223; my translation. [Editors' note: For the English, see *Selected Letters of C. G. Jung, 1901–1906,* ed. Gerhard Adler, trans. R. F. C. Hull (Princeton, N.J.: Princeton University Press, 1984).]

¹⁶ Schwartz-Salant, "On the Interactive Field as the Analytic Object."

¹⁷ Hollis, *The Eden Project,* p. 59.

[18] *Ibid.*

[19] See Willi, *Couples in Collusion.*

[20] Stanley Ruszczynski, "Thinking About and Working with Couples," in *Psychotherapy with Couples: Theory and Practice at the Tavistock Institute of Marital Studies,* ed. Stanley Ruszczynski (London: Karnac, 1993), p. 217.

[21] Hewison, "'Oh Rose, Thou Art Sick!'" p. 690.

[22] Plato, *Symposium,* trans. with an introduction and notes by Alexander Nehemas and Paul Woodruff (Indianapolis, Ind.: Hackett, 1989).

[23] Nathan Schwartz-Salant, *The Mystery of Human Relationship: Alchemy and the Transference of Self* (London: Routledge, 1998).

[24] Jung, "The Psychology of the Transference," §§402–537.

[25] A number of Jungian authors have thoroughly dealt with the subject of archetypal couples. See for example John R. Haule, *Divine Madness: Archetypes of Romantic Love* (Boston: Shambala, 1990); and Verena Kast, *The Nature of Loving: Patterns of Human Relationship,* trans. Boris Matthews (Wilmette, Ill.: Chiron Publications, 1986).

[26] D. Baucom et al., "Empirically Supported Couple and Family Interventions for Marital Distress and Adult Mental Health Problems," *Journal of Consulting and Clinical Psychology* 66, no. 1 (1998): 53–88.

[27] For further ideas on art therapy with couples, see, Walter Feuer, "Gemeinsames Malen aus dem Unbewußten in der Paartherapie," *Analytische Psychologie* 25 (1994): 100–119.

[28] For further ideas on sandplay with couples, see Linde von Keyserlingk, "Sandspieltherapie mit Paaren," *Zeitschrift für Sandspiel-Therapie* 14 (2003): 58–71.

[29] For case studies of sandplay in couples therapy, see Christian Roesler, "Die Verwendung von künstlerischen Ausdrucksformen in der Paartherapie—auf Basis der Psychotherapie nach C. G. Jung," in *Kunsttherapie,* ed. R. Hampe und P. Stalder (Berlin: Frank & Timme, forthcoming).

The Story of Angus, the Celtic God of Dreams
Part 1: Story and Storytelling

Robin van Löben Sels

Angus, the old Celtic god of poetry and love, is also the bringer of dreams. As we all dream, his story speaks to everyone. I've taken much of the story I'll be telling you in Part 2 from a lovely little book called *Dream Angus* by a Scottish author, Alexander McCall Smith.[1] We summon mythic consciousness to listen to all stories, however, because we have been using story—and especially stories like Angus—to manage whatever we have imagined about Heaven and Hell, or before life and after life, since the beginning of time. In that way myth is collective vision, for as living, explanatory stories, myths evoke that level of consciousness where we begin to differentiate between an inner and an outer world and soul appears. Emma Jung described Angus an "elemental being" of the psyche[2] and he continues to be so, for he lives out of values and imaginative depths that are relevant to us and our collective times.

The Greeks called the Celts the Keltoi, "the hidden people," meaning people who had no written records. Early Celts had no religious dogma that we can trace, but apparently everything they did was accompanied by a strong sense of the sacred dimension of all existence. Early Celtic gods were not easily distinguishable from each other, and even today they do not respond easily to analytic examination. Cernunnos, the great horned god pictured on the Gundestrup Cauldron, for example, seems to have been a major deity around which gathered all kinds of images of burgeoning nature, and in Ireland, Dagda (or Dagda the Good, who fathered Angus) may have been another name for Cernunnos.[3]

Between the first telling of myths and what we hear now, Christian, Viking, and Germanic influences poured into Celtic myth and story, coloring them over centuries. You'll hear some of this in the story of Angus, particularly around the fate of the holy man. We are drawn to these stories because they are from and about human beings who were faced with the same essential problems and sorrows and delights as we are today; like us, they journeyed and learned painfully, step by step, to fulfill their considerable potential, and from within and without they were beset by the same dark and violent shadows that we know, too.

MYTH

Before Part 2 and the Story of Angus, let me speak about what I think form the real bones of myth, which is storytelling itself. Just as a personal dream is a small, just-so story in a personal life, myths can be seen as big, collective, Just-So stories that personify in a dynamic, psychological grammar the geo-eco-psychological experience of a particular people in a particular place at a particular time in human history. Myths gather, collect, and swirl around different arenas of human experience. Picture myths as expressions of stationary psychological "storms" emerging from as they also obscure our vision of particular times and places and peoples, looking much like the circling air currents we see on satellite images of current weather conditions.

Myth can also be heard as a kind of collective poetry of the human soul that transmits our human recognition of the mystery of Being by dealing with the fascinating and powerful magic of inner transformation. Myths do not try to *solve* the mystery of our lives, for the task of myth is to make us *notice* the mystery and stop taking things for granted. Myths make us look and question and wonder, for any truth we can know about our lives in this universe has to be elusive, exciting, and mysterious. In pursuing this mystery, as we all do, we are apt to find all that is worth having, *including ourselves*. Thus, myth and storytelling can both free us and encourage us to recognize our original fullness.

STORY AND STORYTELLING

We all tell stories to each other, describing inner and outer experience as best we can. These stories usually describe how things seem to hold together in time. In telling, and in listening, story brings together mind and body, heart and head, arguing for its own significance. A story touches the beginning narrative of our archaic minds, so that listening to a story is almost as important as telling one. The stories we hear form us inwardly as well as outwardly, giving us ways to think about ourselves and the world we inhabit.

When we listen to a story, we tend to hold the characters in silent judgment, investing sympathy here, withholding it there, always alert for recognition, for seeing our own, personal selves reflected across time and space and circumstance. A sudden reflection may bring joy; when nothing occurs, we may feel empty. When imagination falters with the weight of a story that sounds unthinkable, let alone bearable in real life, we may feel afraid. I think of hearing the stories of war veterans or listening to stories told by survivors of great trauma. When this happens, when our minds and hearts stumble at what we hear and imagine, the bones of story weave an undercarriage that supports both speaker and listener, reassuring us not only that may we sometimes help each other bridge the gravitas of personal tragedy but that something else accompanies us as well.

Often when we listen to familiar stories (like biblical stories or fairy tales), our adult minds are suddenly accompanied by our child-minds. The child we were awakens and becomes the child we are. Something similar happens in my consulting room: a person enters, full of an ongoing story plus a background story they've told no one else (at least not in full) and may not know fully themselves. World sorrow resonates behind that voice, for who enters therapy without having been hurt?

In part, my therapeutic endeavor will be to translate that world sorrow into something humanly holdable, personalized feelings that interweave throughout a story that can be experienced and metabolized by the person who tells the story. This happens for each person as it happens for all of us—in the act of hearing oneself *tell* a personal story, for we have to learn about ourselves by listening to ourselves as well as to each other. This necessarily personal story will touch my sympathetic nature and make me aware (again) of how unsympathetic the world can be, that world to which all of us are constantly exposed. The simple humanity of the personal story will persuade me that even solitude and distress are credible and right and necessary, despite evidence of wrongness all around. I will feel all over again how deeply solitude and despair are woven into the fabric of human Being.

Our present society is fairly good about acknowledging (at least verbally) First Nations and Indigenous Peoples. But in order to acknowledge a first language of all people, a primary language of perception, recognition, instinct, affect, and emotion, we have to recognize the reality of the psyche. Many of us find it hard enough to translate what we experience into words, and when we are emerging from inner space it is even harder, so that much of what we see and experience is bound to remain unconscious and never told. Some of us may feel that our lives have happened to us ruthlessly and without mercy. Many of us may feel that from one moment to the next we hardly know what is going on, let alone what it all means.

So storytelling is not a luxury. It is as necessary as bread. We cannot imagine ourselves without stories, and without *telling* stories, because each of us, each self, *is* a story. As a dream is to our waking life, so is a story to our reality. Even our ordinary daily conversation asks for story: What's happening, we say, or how are you, or how was your day? What do we desire with these questions? Answers, yes, but also we are saying, "Tell me a story that tells me about you, that pulls me out of myself and connects me to another, to the world." Just as a brain can't function without clearing its circuits during sleep, we cannot contemplate and analyze our lives without living some of the time in the world of the deep imagination, where we sort and refine the random events of our lives into personal stories.

Thus, in my office, I listen to stories with an awareness that wells up from a shared silence. Oddly enough, shared silence makes possible a stronger narrative of individual life. It seems to stimulate internal states of the imagination. In silence, memory stirs. When silence needs words, I sometimes say "Tell me more" or "Try to put it into words." My child-mind folds the story into my memory and my psychoanalytic mind ponders what I hear, but something else participates too, along with my deep appreciation of the seemingly infinite variables of the human condition, not to mention sheer awe at what people experience in our struggle to embody time, space, and personhood.

Though psyche seems beyond the reach of sense, in part psyche comes to me *through* my senses. The psyche of my brother or sister may remain as far from my *direct* reach as the psyches of my beloved animals, but beneath an ever-present chorus of body language (my own and that of the other person) that continually demands my close attention, here are ways I track the elusive soul: within myself I try to stay aware of something that is not a tangible part of my body as I feel and experience the psyche of another person *because I am told of it*—psyche and soul enter my awareness as I hear and understand the words of someone else's story. I also depend on my own imaginative capacity and a kind of continual experience of emotional commonality, an original (in the sense of first or early) perception that simply by being human, all of us belong to a single species of creaturely being.

I want to emphasize that the idea of a silent listener, the idea of someone who holds silence so that others can speak their true selves into it, is an extraordinary development. A therapist's capacity to hold silence differs from a confessor's silence in religious life, for example, for the function of confessors, spiritual directors, gurus, sheiks, and teachers tends to be explicitly directive or instructive and is often judgmental. In theory, at least, and at the deepest level of being, therapists do not teach, direct, judge, or instruct. Rather, therapists and analysts try to create and hold a free silence in which subjects of the therapeutic process struggle to find themselves, name themselves, accept themselves, and, eventually (again, in theory) even come to love themselves.

So in part, stories are acts we make against loneliness. Telling a story is an appeal to community, a bet on the possibility of spanning the gulf that separates you from me and me from you. Our stories illustrate varieties of the human condition in order to bring more of that condition, of *what it is like to be human,* into the light of conscious insight. It seems that whenever *something is like* something else, we have to wrap it in story. Storytelling thus expands our sense of being as well as our self-knowledge, and in the absence of honest storytelling we may well find ourselves alone with the solitary beating of our own hearts.

As necessary as story is, however, we don't always use it well. We all know people who recite stories not to connect to themselves or to others but to keep others at arm's length. And here is a memorable definition of hell: being stuck in one's own story and unable to move on. At times like this, unconsciousness is paramount. All who tell stories must descend to where their stories are kept, and it is terribly easy to be captured and held immobile by the past. Perhaps this happens so often because in reality the big things like truth and beauty, love and birth, death and loss and pain *happen* to us.

We *undergo* these Big Things, and we have little to do with avoiding them or bringing them about. We are not in charge of the Big Things. The things we *are* in charge of are small, really—like crafting shared meaning or human consciousness or learning to relate to each other instead of merging or how to participate in each other's lives or how to love.

Should we discover that we are locked into this kind of hell, we can thank our lucky stars for whatever experience we've been able to garner of the fairly recent language and discipline of psychotherapy, despite how difficult and arduous (and costly) it has been. Perhaps everyone here knows what it is like to "fall into a complex" and work your way out of it again, usually with another person's help (if only for perspective.) Or how about falling into one's "basic fault": *that* feels like falling into the Grand Canyon and having to climb out all by yourself.

The point is, however, that when we come close to the things that break us down, we may touch upon the things that break us open. And every so often this is the point of healing, for only when we tell our personal story can we leave that story behind. What remains with us then is an experience of hidden wholeness that feels alive again and unbroken: hope arrives, and the potential dawns for whole-heartedness in the days ahead, along with—at the very least—self-acceptance.

BEYOND PERSONAL STORY

Another important point is that we have to mature enough to emerge from encapsulation in our personal story to develop a more open-minded or philosophical or psychological or spiritual point of view. Just as a cultural myth reflects a particular time and place and people in which it came to life, changing cultural dress and color around an unchanging core of universal human desire, fear, and longing, our personal stories change as we change, centering new perspectives and attitudes on a core of irreducible personal experience. We uncover our mythic selves (impersonal but true) only as we strengthen our personal selves. This means that we discover unconscious personal myths only by moving beyond them. And moving beyond the confines of personal story is what then frees us to rejoin as *personal selves* the bigger stories of our culture, whatever those stories may be.

Making and telling stories, then, works in an elementary narrative nucleus that has accompanied our species for thousands of years. That narrative consists primarily of going into and returning from the beyond. Thus, to "narrate" means to speak here and now, but to speak with an authority that derives from having been (literally and/or figuratively) *there and then*. Personal stories always straddle these two worlds, too: this is a distinctive trait of our human species. And cultural myths like the story of Angus work this same theme on a larger scale: participation in the world of the living and the world of the dead or the human world and the animal world or visible and invisible realms or the dream world and the world of waking. (Listen for these two worlds as you listen to the story of Angus.) To enter the narrative of these larger stories helps us enter a bigger world.

IMAGE AND PERSONIFICATION

When we experience personifications like those who will come to life in the story of Angus, we look at and participate in intellectual and emotional energies that ignite clusters of fused ideas that present themselves in images here and now. Like the images of our dreams, personifications are anything but two-dimensional. The imagery of dreams and myths are like icons that offer an image through which powerful energies stream and penetrate us. These images participate in our lives, and we participate in theirs. We experience dream and myth differently, as if the eyes of these personifications meet the gaze of we who gaze upon them. In other words, Angus and those who form the milieu of his story will join us as we listen, igniting our imaginations and our dreams.

As mentioned earlier, personifications of psychic energy seem to happen mostly when feeling is at stake or when values need emphasizing. Most of us find it easier to love a person, for example, than to love a principle or an abstract concept. I will be suggesting that Angus personifies our *feeling desire* to bend our attention toward a dawning sense of self and soul that not only happens through loving and dreaming but, more importantly, happens through submitting to the experience of mystery that is inherent in these two domains.

Angus personifies a kind of consciousness that I call "participating consciousness" that we can all experience and that we always enter as we love and dream, a consciousness that we may come to value so deeply that we recognize and seek to cultivate it consciously.[4] After all is said and done, all of us submit to the mysteries of loving and dreaming; these are not activities that we willfully do. Angus personifies someone who values and loves the mysteries of Being, and his story unfolds an important collective dream that all of us share: the idea that the mysterious aspects of loving and dreaming shall forever remain beyond our comprehension and control.

NOTES

[1] Alexander McCall Smith, *Dream Angus: The Celtic God of Dreams* (Edinburgh, Scotland: Canongate, 2006).

[2] Emma Jung, "The Anima as Elemental Being," in *Animus and Anima: Two Papers,* trans. Hildegard Nagel (1951; repr., Dallas, Tex.: Spring Publications, 1985), p. 50.

[3] Moyra Caledecott, *Women in Celtic Myth: Tales of Extraordinary Women from the Ancient Celtic Tradition* (Rochester, Vt.: Destiny Books, 1992), p. 4. Wikipedia tells us that Cernunnos (also Cernenus and Cern) is associated with male horned animals, especially the stag and the stag-horned snake, and thus with fertility. His antlered image was widespread among ancient Celtic lands of Western Europe.

[4] For more on the notion of participating consciousness, see Part 2.

The Story of Angus, the Celtic God of Dreams Part 2:
Angus: Poet, Lover, and Bringer of Dreams

Robin van Löben Sels

Now to Angus and his story, rooted in a Celtic world peopled by mortals and gods beyond concrete memory. Medieval versions of this myth exist for the purists among us, but as Alexander McCall Smith suggests, "Earlier texts are themselves reworked versions of things passed from mouth to mouth, embroidered and mixed up in the process."[1] Myths live in the present and are there for us to play with and live within. In our times Angus inspired not only W. B. Yeats's "The Song of Wandering Aengus" but also the lilting Scottish lullaby "Dream Angus."[2]

Like many mythologies, Celtic mythology embraces the notion of parallel universes, a real world and another world. The motif of two interpenetrating worlds parallels intimate ways that our sentient lives and the unconscious interact in ordinary life, so we can appreciate how an attack upon one or the other threatens a sense of balance and awakens a need for redress, whether in the fields of everyday emotion or the enchanted lands of mythology.

The Newgrange monument on the River Boyne in Ireland is both the birthplace and the palace of Angus and his father, Dagda the Good, father of the gods and patron of the Druids. Boann, a water goddess, is Angus's mother. In the myth, Dagda "borrows" Angus's mother from her husband Elcmar and causes the sun to remain overhead for nine months so that Boann can gestate a child without Elcmar's realizing that more than one day has passed.[3]

In most versions of this story Angus is relatively benign. Young, handsome, and playful, he constellates love and dreams wherever he goes.

From childhood, Angus personifies two mediating functions of the psyche: introverted dreaming and extroverted loving. More important, Angus presides over the *mysteries* of these two functions. More basic, profound human experiences are hard to imagine (birth and death, perhaps, and giving birth), for all of us dream and love, and I suspect that dreaming and loving have something to do with being human in the first place.

Angus inhabits what the Irish call a "thin place,"[4] where visible and invisible worlds meet and intermingle, elements of Being link and communicate and exchange essences, and dreams not only disturb our sleep and expand our consciousness but speak to us in a language of real experience and real news, making us laugh and cry and reminding us that we are not alone. Angus arrives, and dreams appear. The membrane separating two worlds becomes transparent as dreams pour through, revealing a new population of creaturely beings.[5]

Dagda's people were the Tuatha Dé Danann, the People of Dana. As father and chief, Dagda possessed a huge cauldron that never ran out of food and a great club with which he slew many men with a single blow. Because he was a master of music, his harp flew through the air to him at his command.

A bit like Zeus in his mating habits, Dagda is not above disguising himself in order to have what he desires. Smith weaves a fine story about how Dagda came to father Angus, who delights all who come across him. In many ways, writes Smith,

> this was Dagda's greatest achievement, that he gave us this fine
> boy, who brought dreams to people, and who was loved by birds
> and people equally and who still is. You may spot him skipping
> across the heather, his bag of dreams by his side, and the sight
> of him, just the sight, may be enough to make you fall in love.
> For he is also a dispenser of love, an Eros. (pp. 2–3)

So how does Dagda, powerful god and leader of warriors, have a dreamy son who falls in love and charms birds? To explain the nature of Angus we turn to his mother, Boann. "Water spirits are gentle," writes Smith. "Their sons are handsome and have a sense of fun; they sparkle and dart about, just like water . . . the most playful of the elements"(p. 3). Boann, shy and gentle and kind, lives in a river "both great and small." You might hardly notice her, says Smith, except for a "ripple on the surface of the water, or a splash of the sort made by an otter or some other small creature slipping into the water, hardly enough to make you turn your head and think of investigating further" (p. 4).

Boann has fallen in love with a holy man who often visits her river and tells her stories about his childhood and a white dog he once had, a dog with a brave heart that did many fine deeds. The holy man spends hours sinking beneath the surface of the river, breathing underwater while he meditates, so he also inhabits two worlds (above and below), just as a water goddess links the elements of water and earth.

> Boann was pleased that the holy man had come to live under her river. . . . She did not want any gods to hear about him. It was not unknown for gods to become jealous of holy men, or possessive of them, and she did not want someone to kill her holy man or take him away. (p. 7)

But eventually, hearing of Boann's beauty, Dagda comes round to investigate: "Nobody would know that Dagda was coming, because he was the wind and the rain and the clouds in the sky. Dagda was Ireland, and Ireland was all about. He was Scotland too, and lands beyond that" (p. 8).

As Dagda approaches where he knows the water nymph lives, he hears beautiful song "like the sound of running water" and he sees Boann singing to the holy man, who has just emerged from his meditations. Immediately Dagda is jealous and decides to get rid of him. When Boann goes to visit Elcmar, Dagda reaches into the river, pulls out the holy man, and holds him high in the sky so he cannot breathe. The holy man drowns in the air, just "as a fish dies in [thin] air," with his eyes wide and "his skin turned to scales. The light is silver on those scales—silver and gold, like the scales of a trout when it is taken from sweet water" (p. 9).

Dagda throws the body of the holy man, which cartwheels across the sky. (There should be a constellation named for this story, but I haven't found it.) Perhaps in the flying body of the drowning holy man we glimpse how frail over-spiritualized personal feeling can become, tossed high and dry when primitive erotic energy erupts through the religious imagination.

Dagda now puts on the holy man's clothes and waits for Boann to return. He calls from under the river in the voice of the holy man and Boann rises from the reeds. (Again, the voice of one world hidden within another.) Dagda holds Boann in his arms and she conceives a child.

Secretly, say some of the tales, Boann is pleased, for she is really in love with Dagda too, although she is afraid of what Elcmar will think if she is seen in the company of such a powerful god. Yet Dagda does not stay. Returning to his own life (and his own wife), Dagda laughs so loudly that people are frightened, thinking they hear thunder.

When Dagda leaves, Boann becomes angry, missing her holy man. But she comforts herself with the thought of her coming child. Knowing she must hide the child so that Dagda does not steal him, Boann weaves a basket of rush. She gives birth with "a great cry," startling from nearby trees "a great flock of birds that wheel and dip through the morning sky," and she places Angus in his basket to float on the edge of the river (p. 16). Boann watches over Angus and is never far away. Four brightly colored little birds (called "kisses") hovered around Angus's head at birth, and now they circle the infant as he lies in his basket. And everywhere nearby people begin to dream.

Dagda has messengers, and he eventually hears about the child Boann has hidden. When Dagda seizes Angus, Boann struggles, but she is only water: "She pleaded with Dagda not to take her child, but her pleading was no more sound than that a river makes when it crackles between stones. . . . She wept, but her tears were no more than the soft rain" (p. 20).

Angus spends only one night in Dagda's household, where he sleeps in the kitchen next to the wonderful never-empty cauldron with the women who keep the fires burning. That night everyone dreams vivid dreams, and they wake up "wide-eyed with wonder at the things they had seen in these dreams, astonishing things, wonderful things" (p. 36).

Dagda dreams too. Even as a babe in arms, Angus reveals his qualities. In his dream, Dagda saw a fair-haired boy knocking on the door of his house. The boy led him gently outside, where Dagda was alone without his men to guard him. He did not have his cauldron, either, or his great club, which suddenly went all weak and useless. This nightmare awakens Dagda, and he has had enough. When he appears in the kitchen the next morning, he orders the women to take Angus to the house of Midir, another son, where he is to be raised as Midir's son rather than Dagda's own.

Midir receives the baby and two kind women are given the job of looking after Angus. They too dream intensely and awaken elated, as if they had seen things that only the gods could see. And the little birds that accompany Angus wherever he goes dream little bird-dreams. The women hear them, rustling in the leaves outside the windows.

Angus grows quickly, learning to walk and run. He does not seem to care about danger. Midir's great hunting dogs become quiet near Angus and lie down at his feet. Midir grows proud of Angus and never tells him that he is Dagda's son, while Angus grows to love Midir's real son like a brother. But when he is eight years old, Angus dreams that he will lose his brother, and he wakens in tears.

One day a schoolmate taunts Angus, telling him that he doesn't even know his true father and mother. Angus storms off to Midir:

> "Who is my true father?" he asked. "It's not you, is it?"
> [And Midir answered him truthfully,] "No, I am not your
> father." . . .
>   "Then I must find my him," said Angus. "I must claim
> what is mine." (p. 62)

And Angus sets off. When he finds Dagda (who is very surprised),
Angus announces, "'I am your son.' . . . 'So you are,' said Dagda. 'You are
welcome in this house. Oh yes. Yes'" (p. 64). Then Angus turns to his father
and says,

> "Since I am your son . . . you will surely let me take over
> your kingdom someday." But Dagda was immortal, and this is
> not possible. . . .
>   Dagda was about to say, *oh yes,* but he stopped himself in
> time and shook his head. "That is impossible," he said. "I am
> the One. That is me. Only me."
>   Angus smiled. . . . "I only wish to have this place for night
> and day," [he] said.
>   [Dagda, hearing] *a night and day,* saw no reason why he
> should not allow [this little thing]. Then, when the boy had
> had his chance to be ruler for a short time he could be dispatched
> on a long errand and would probably never return.
>   Dagda nodded. "Yes," he said. "Oh yes." (pp. 65–66; italics
> in original)

Perhaps Dagda is looking forward to a brief outing, a sabbatical from
his responsibilities. Perhaps he will go cattle rustling. "Good-bye, father,"
Angus calls. "I shall be back tomorrow," says Dagda (p. 67).

And Angus turns to the people and tells them that there will be a fine
dance that night, with music and wonderful food. The musicians play until
dawn, until everyone, small gods muddled up with ordinary people, sleeps
a wonderful sleep of exhaustion and happiness. As they sleep, Angus goes
around the room, stopping here and there, leaving a dream with this one
and a dream with that one, generous wherever he goes.

By the time Dagda comes back from his outing, everyone is awake,
talking to one another about the fine sleep and the wonderful dreams they
have had. Dagda is highly annoyed, for he doesn't approve of dances. But
when he orders everybody out and threatens to smite people with his club,
no one moves. They simply look to Angus, who says, "No."

> "Nobody need leave. For I am now in charge of this
> place." . . .
>   "You are very mistaken," [says Dagda]. "You were in charge

only for a day and a night. That is what I agreed to." . . .

[Angus smiles sweetly again, still gentle:] "You agreed to
my being in charge for day and night," he corrected. "And since
night follows day and day follows night and will always do so,
I am in charge forever. Is that not so?"

Angus turned to the people and small gods. And with one
voice they shouted, "Yes. Oh yes." (pp. 68–69)

And with that, the power of Dagda is broken. He shuffles out of the
hall, cursing his son, and goes to another place far away, leaving Angus
in possession of everything. Dagda's archaic consciousness is baffled
and defeated. Angus, his son, introduces a mythic differentiation: day
and night and night following day—not yet linear time, but different
enough from the archaic, magical realm into which he was born that Dagda's
world gives way.

Angus's Love

We've heard of the little birds that accompanied Angus and circled his head
and the great cry and wheeling of the birds in the sky. Birds feature again
in Angus's courtship of Caer, a beautiful woman who appears to him in
his dreams and sings music that enchants him. Caer becomes as real to
Angus as if he were awake, and Angus knows that she is the person he
wishes to be with. But Caer keeps disappearing, as dreams do, and although
Angus dreams of her over and over, never does she stay.

Angus grows so ill with longing that Fergne, the greatest healer in
Ireland, is summoned to his side. Knowing at once that Angus is sick from
lost love, Fergne summons Boann from her river and Dagda the Good
from his distraction and asks them to help. But Boann can't find the
girl and Dagda can't find the girl, and finally Dagda turns to Bov the
Red,[6] highly skilled in all mysteries and enchantments. Bov sends
messengers throughout the land to look for the girl Angus describes, and
after a year, Bov finds the visionary maiden at the Lake of the Dragon's
Mouth and takes Angus to her.

Caer, too, is of divine descent. Her father, Ethal, is one of the Tuatha
Dé Danann. Once Caer is found, however, family difficulties arise. Dagda
has to intervene, to persuade (read *threaten*) Caer's father to give the girl
to Angus. When Caer's father finally agrees, he warns Dagda that the girl
is far more powerful than he, so she, too, has to give consent. To make
matters worse, Caer spends alternate years as a wild swan. When Angus
goes to the Lake of the Dragon's Mouth he calls Caer by name, and although
she recognizes the sound, she tells Angus she will come ashore only if he

comes another time. On the feast of Samhain, Angus returns to the lake to find Caer swimming among 150 swans now linked altogether with a slender golden chain. He recognizes Caer, taller than the others and of an unearthly beauty, and when Angus renews his love, Caer comes to the shore and kisses him.

As he explains who he is, Angus finds *himself* transforming into a swan. As he raises his arms they become wings—huge, magnificent, and white to the pinions. Taking this as consent—from the gods? from Caer? from himself?—Angus plunges into the lake to join his love. Caer sees him, turning her neck as swans do, and Angus goes to her. As two swans, Caer and Angus fall asleep on the water.

When they awaken, Caer agrees to marry Angus.

> Together they rose above the waters of the lake and circled its shore several times [to seal his promise to protect her]. The sound of their beating wings was the sound of a heartbeat, the sound of blood in the veins, the very sound of life. (p. 147)

Finally, singing a magical duet, they fly away north to the Boyne, uttering a music so divine that all who hear it are lulled to sleep for three days and nights. They will always be lovers as swans and as man and woman, and this is how Angus becomes a receiver of dreams and love as well.

ABOUT THIS STORY

Situating these figures in the Jungian world, Emma Jung suggests that because Caer appears to Angus in a dream, she is destined for him and he cannot live without her, his anima. Angus submits to his anima's conditions and even takes on her form, becoming a swan himself. "He attempts to meet her in her own element," Emma writes, ". . . in order to make her permanently his—conduct which should also prove of value psychologically, in relating to the anima. The magical song of the two swans is an expression of the fact that two beings of opposite nature, which yet belong together, have now in harmonious concord been united."[7]

I don't fully agree with Emma Jung's comments because I fret at the phrase *"in order to make her permanently his,"* which suggests making a living person a possession. Emma casts Angus's participation in Caer's nature so forcefully that Angus's pursuit of Caer appears as a means to an end, even if a psychological end. I suspect that love is more persuasive than power and possessiveness with the anima, as with humans. But I appreciate Emma's recognition that this myth is not a tale of redemption.

The story of Angus is a *coniunctio* myth, conjoining land and sky, river and stone, male and female, human and animal, the world of daylight and the world of dreams. This is a myth of sacred marriage, and, like all *coniunctio* motifs, it concerns the transformative aspect of new beginnings.

The song of Angus is a song of life in the body and the body in the world. It is not a song of meaning but a song of love. Angus displays remarkable virtue in his attitude toward his beloved and her chosen form of life. Remember that Caer was not enchanted into becoming a swan, as in other tales. She is not an elemental creature in need of rescue or redemption. Nor can she be *made* to be part of Angus, coerced into capitulation. Before she met Angus, Caer *chose* to spend half her life identified with the "more-than-human" world,[8] and Angus follows her lead. Angus comes from a line of seers and prophets unprejudiced toward the irrational and is wonderfully responsive to influence from the other side of consciousness. Rather than trying to redeem Caer from swanhood, which would involve heroic action of some kind, Angus joins her and becomes a swan himself. How rare is that?

This is not a story where behind animal form is concealed a higher being that must be redeemed before the hero unites with her. Were this so, Caer would be part of an original state of unity—a human princess, perhaps—whose wholeness, eroded by enchantment, has to be re-created. Redemption stories point toward a primal condition that is somehow destroyed, either by the sins of men or the envy of the gods, and this ancient concept forms the basis of many of our religious and philosophic systems: the biblical doctrine of man's fall, Plato's originally spherical primal being split into halves, and the Gnostic Sophia, imprisoned in matter. But it does not appear in the story of Angus.

Perhaps because we are on Celtic earth here, the realm of fairy does not have the fearful character that it possesses elsewhere. It is not a kingdom of the dead, for example. Caer is the daughter of a father who openly acknowledges that she is more powerful that he and that her consent is what matters. Caer represents the immensely important possibility of *both-and* rather than *either/or*—life that is both day and night, conscious and unconscious, both fully human and fully more than human. Caer is not *half* of anything at all. Loving and joining her—one year a swan, one year a human—Angus expands his innate capacity for empathy, sympathy, kinship with another *and* with a wider (as well as *wilder*) natural world.

Although he undergoes many tribulations of the divine child, Angus appears at home in himself from early on and is not driven into heroics. Dagda's defeat comes not through his son's heroism but through his own distracted misunderstanding. Representing a link between wildly different elements—his father a warrior-god, his mother a water goddess—Angus might have been more "of two natures," for there is something of the hero in him *and* something of the divine child. But Angus behaves differently.

Angus has an inner life, for one thing, which is unusual for heroes in the tales I know. For another, Angus participates in the life he constellates rather than overcoming or transforming it. As a giver of dreams Angus also *has* dreams; as one who inspires love and adoration in others, Angus also loves and adores someone other than himself. Seldom does such behavior grace the heroic quest, and implicit in the transfer of Dagda's kingdom to Angus and the marriage of Angus and Caer is the transformation of the heroic attitude.

ANGUS AS SHAMAN

Clearly the story of Angus is not moral or didactic. Instead, in the intensity of dreams and love, Angus personifies a shamanic vocation. Always and everywhere shamans tell us that the "fire in the head" means an illuminating vision of other realities that become a source of enlightenment.[9] In many respects Angus's journey represents a classic shamanic soul journey illuminated by a powerful imagination. As is true with any shaman, the beliefs and expectations of Angus's own nature and surrounding culture shaped the content of his dreams, meaning that although he may not have enkindled the fire in his head, like shamans everywhere, Angus collected the kindling for that fire from the beliefs and values of what he knew: from rivers and lakes, from colored birds and wild swans, and from the astounding beauty of the world in which he lived.

These elements kindle the imaginative soul in all of us, wherever we live, whether we are shamans or not. They remind us that the shamanic world of spirit and power is always poised to break through ordinary consciousness—while taking a walk, while fishing for trout, while lighting a fire for breakfast. Lighting a fire in the morning was when I imagine Jung found time not only to listen to the many voices of the kettle's song but also to talk to his pots and pans while he made himself breakfast in his lakeside tower at Bollingen.[10]

The story of Angus speaks to us because primary values—the experience of an "other" world and the importance of dreams—exist in our psychological culture, too. Out of personal experience of the reality of the psyche, trauma, complex psychology, and archetypal energy, analytical psychology forges a similar grammar. Like Angus, we look to our dreams. Like Angus, we journey *in* rather than out, *down* rather than up. For us, too, spiritual depth comes from the earth and our animal selves: there we find the treasure we seek and need, alive and potent, left by all our ancestors, the Celts among them.

We, too, seek to rejoin the unconscious and the natural world, not to save it (as once we thought) or save ourselves from it. And just as we need dialogue with the unconscious, we desperately need dialogue with the natural world. Caer and Angus, living their love, enter a bigger life.[11] Participating in the shape-shifting currents of the earth and its creaturely inhabitants, Angus and Caer assume their place in what we call the soul of the world, the *anima mundi*.

So What to Make of Angus?

I think of Angus as a kind of god of subjectivity, meaning experience that is known only by the person subjected to it—a dream, an experience of great beauty, an experience of love, a religious experience. We *undergo* subjective experience; we aren't in charge. Angus is the god of the mystery of this kind of experience. When we close down our subjective side—or feel it crumple in trauma or despair—we lose our impulse to make something of our experience, whatever it is. We lose our subjective capacity to invest the reality we know with energy, emotion, and imagination. We lose the capacity to make meaning of what happens to us. Jung suggests that our ego falls into the unconscious and gets assimilated to the Self. When we do not respond to subjective experience, we experience the Self as the inert weight of fate. Sometimes we love our fate; at other times, we cry aloud with dismay and grief. Both attitudes indicate weakness of subjectivity, which has to stand up and make its own meaning. Otherwise we do not inhabit our own life, and when we forget to make a narrative thread, we forget to tell our stories. Then we need Angus, who loves and values subjective experience and lives it fully. Angus gladly suffers his personal experience of life.

And Angus always seems to have a life of his own. People love him because in his presence they feel themselves take on substance. The people around Angus don't serve his inner life as much as they suddenly glimpse their own. They take interest in themselves and the mysteries of the inner world as well as in the mysterious nature of the world around them.

Guarding and loving mystery as he does, it is no surprise that Angus is also a god of poets, artists, and storytelling. He serves those who look to language and use it less to find meaning than to explore or express our precious human cultural heritage, which is both religious and deeply creative. This heritage, glimpsed in poem or story, song or painting, may feel obscure: often we barely make out the message, even as our hearts beat more rapidly. Then Angus may send a dream that reassures us that language is not well designed to operate in the domain of mystery; it does what it can, but language never tells the whole story. Images and dreams are what stretch our sentience. Angus is a god for those who, like Yeats, believe that we may embody truth but we can never *know* it.[12]

Angus and Caer bring to mind images of an old alchemist working side by side with his *soror mystica,* or the brother-sister pairing of equals commonly sought in couples today. Some evolution of the psyche has taken place over the past century, and perhaps we glimpse it here. Can it be that a *coniunctio* story better suits the "spirit of our times?" As the poet A. R. Ammon has said, "If anything will level with you, water will."[13]

Angus symbolizes and constellates that of which we are all capable— a desire toward subjective experience that honors the mysteries in what Jung describes as a doubled effort toward "consciousness plus a full participation in life"; that is, a capacity to develop and experience participating consciousness, a consciousness that links personal and collective life, the personal unconscious and the collective dream.[14]

Does Angus personify a possible *coniunctio* or intersection of the Spirit that links "the spirit of the times" and the "spirit of the depths" here and now, bringing our attention to a consciousness that bridges the chasm between the two, more easily encompassing the terrific tension of split within the spirit that Jung tells us that he experienced in his time?[15] In *The Red Book,* Jung details how stretched he personally felt between the spirit of the times and the spirit of the depths as he strove to "hold the opposites," linking his experience of consciousness and the unconscious, and how deeply he suffered as he found his way.[16]

If this transformation of consciousness seems possible to us now, then let us say that Angus stands at the threshold of the psyche whenever we tell our personal story to someone, whether that person is our therapist, our mate, our child, or a stranger on the street. Let us say that Angus comes to you every night with another installment of your individuation story, the dream from which you have yet to awaken, the one that slips from your grasp as you open your eyes, the dream that haunts you even after you write it down. Angus brings the dream you remember, years after it happened, the one that is suddenly full of new meaning.

Fathered by an irrational eruption of primitive instinct and mothered by the element that makes up almost 90 percent of our human body, Angus is human in dreaming and loving and loss and more than human in his kinship with animals and birds. I think of Angus as the awakening energy of our mirror neurons,[17] those links of our being that happen at lightning speed within and among us as we live and work together, links that allow empathy and the exchange of stories as we carefully feel our ways into each other's lives. Whether we understand birds and music as spirit and creativity or as psyche and soul doesn't matter: Angus's kinship with all creatures and the more-than-human world defines soulfulness and participation in the *anima mundi.*[18]

Angus brings dreams of love and dreams of those we love. He brings access to a world of unimaginable beauty and awe. He is also the god we acknowledge when our projections onto each other lie in shards around our feet and the transfixing illusion of mutuality falls away. When this happens, we are left with the dark mystery of ineffable subjective experience. Or perhaps we are *indeed* alone before a fleeting experience of extraordinary beauty that we know marks us forever yet is impossible to convey.

Angus marks the borderlands of religious experience, too. Here, the dreams Angus brings reassure us that what we love can be believed in but not possessed. We may have to let go of that which we love in order to digest the experience of love. Angus also shows us that we don't control who or what we love—or when or why—and that we can't know ahead of time what events in our world will become so definitive that they mark us indelibly with a personally engraved experience of who and what we are. These dreams-in-the-world, as I call them, form the unique watercourse of our individuality, marking the spaces where the clear waters of Boann have opened our hearts along the river-road we take through time.[19]

Paradoxically, we are enmeshed yet singular. We live experience that cannot be shared or given away, nevertheless we seek each other to tell. We cannot live alone. And so we speak and we tell our stories, and from time to time Dagda erupts into our lives in an irrational burst, breaking domestication and tranquility and religious tradition to smithereens. (Remember the flying holy man, drowning in air?)

And so Boann surrounds our hearts and our minds and nurtures them and flows and encompasses all that ensues with the fluidity of river water shining in the sun. And Angus is born, and born again, wanderer, dreamer, shaman, and poet, lover of the world most of all. We are such stuff as dreams are made on, says Shakespeare's Prospero. And Angus sends the dreams.

NOTES

[1] Alexander McCall Smith, *Dream Angus: The Celtic God of Dreams* (Edinburgh, Scotland: Canongate, 2006), p. xiv. Hereafter cited in the text with page numbers.

[2] Yeats's poem "The Song of Wandering Aengus" was first published in *The Wind among the Reeds* (New York: J. Lane, 1899). The poem is available at Bartleby.com, http://www.bartleby.com/146/9.html. The words to the lullaby "Dream Angus" are at the website Traditional Scottish Songs, http://www.rampantscotland.com/songs/blsongs_dream.htm.

[3] Patricia Monaghan, *The Encyclopedia of Celtic Mythology and Folklore* (New York: Checkmark Books, 2008), p. 21. In mythic time, as in archaic and magical time, there is only a kind of intermittent "now," with long stretches of unconsciousness in between. Dagda moves in mythic time, illustrating how one world can encapsulate another and none may be the wiser. Note this, because later Dagda is so self-absorbed that he cannot hear Angus clearly when his son asks for his inheritance. Then Dagda believes as blindly in one day's passing as Elcmar did, although this costs him his kingdom.

[4] The term "thin places" designates highly charged places (and times) where visible and invisible worlds meet. The metaphor arose in the context of the Celtic Christianity that flourished in Ireland and parts of Scotland, Wales, and northern England beginning in the fifth century. See Marcus J. Borg, *The Heart of Christianity: Rediscovering a Life of Faith* (San Francisco: HarperSanFrancisco, 1989), p. 155.

[5] Jung says that a dream is not a façade or a disguise but "a living situation . . . like an animal with feelers, or many umbilical cords. . . . We are moved by dreams, they express us and we express them, and there are coincidences connected with them." C. G. Jung, *Dream Analysis: Notes of the Seminar Given in 1928–1930,* ed. William McGuire, Bollingen Series XCIX (London: Routledge, 1984), p. 44.

[6] In some versions Bov the Red is Dagda's brother; in others Bov is another of Dagda's sons and Angus's half-brother.

[7] Emma Jung, "The Anima as Elemental Being," in *Animus and Anima: Two Papers,* trans. Hildegard Nagel (1951; repr., Dallas, Tex.: Spring Publications, 1985), pp. 50–51.

[8] The term "more than human" comes from an excellent book: David Abrams, *The Spell of the Sensuous: Perception and Language in a More-Than-Human World* (New York: Pantheon, 1996).

⁹ Tom Cowan, *Fire in the Head: Shamanism and the Celtic Spirit* (New York: HarperSanFrancisco, 1993), p. 8.

¹⁰ C. G. Jung, *Memories, Dreams, Reflections,* ed. Aniela Jaffé, trans. Richard and Clara Winston (New York: Vintage Books, 1961), p. 229.

¹¹ "We today are also looking for certain other values," says Jung. "We seek life, not efficiency, and this seeking of ours is directly against the collective ideals of our times." C. G. Jung, "Lecture 13, 15 June 1925," in *Analytical Psychology: Notes of the Seminar Given in 1925,* ed. William McGuire (Princeton, N.J.: Princeton University Press, 1989), p. 68.

¹² "Man can embody truth, but he cannot know it." W. B. Yeats to Lady Elizabeth Pelham, 4 January 1939, in *The Letters of W. B. Yeats,* ed. Allan Wade (London: Rupert Hart-Davies, 1954), p. 322.

¹³ A. R. Ammon, "If Anything Will Level with You Water Will," in *Collected Poems 1951–1971* (New York: W. W. Norton, 1972), p. 290.

¹⁴ See my work on participating consciousness in "When A Body Meets A Body," in *Spring 72: Body & Soul. Honoring Marion Woodman. A Journal of Archetype and Culture* (New Orleans, La.: Spring Journal, 2005), pp. 236–242.

¹⁵ See Robin van Löben Sels, "Ancestors and Spirits of the Dead," *Quadrant: The Journal of the C. G. Jung Foundation* 40, no. 2 (Summer 2010): 81–94.

¹⁶ See C. G. Jung, *The Red Book: Liber Novus,* ed. Sonu Shamdasani, trans. Mark Kyburz and John Peck (New York: W. W. Norton, 2009).

¹⁷ And our collective awareness of these neurons. See V. S. Ramachandran and Sandra Blakeslee, *Phantoms in the Brain: Probing the Mysteries of the Human Mind,* foreword by Oliver Sacks (New York: HarperCollins, 1998).

¹⁸ "Hemmed round by rationalistic walls, we are cut off from the eternity of nature," writes Jung about himself and his (and still our) time. "Analytical psychology seeks to break through these walls by digging up again the fantasy-images of the unconscious which our rationalism has rejected. These images lie beyond the walls; they are part of the nature *in us,* which apparently lies buried in our past and against which we have barricaded ourselves behind the walls of reason." C. G. Jung, "Analytical Psychology and *Weltanschauung*" (1928), in *The Collected Works of C. G. Jung,* vol. 8, *The Structure and Dynamics of the Psyche,* ed. and trans. Gerhard Adler and R. F. C. Hull (Princeton, N. J.: Princeton University Press, 1970), §739.

¹⁹ Robin van Löben Sels, *A Dream in the World: Poetics of Soul in Two Women, Modern and Medieval* (Hove & New York: Brunner-Routledge, 2003).

Dreaming in Gersau, Switzerland
(Jungian Odyssey, 23–25 May 2010)

Robin van Löben Sels

igure 1 is an illustration or kind of map of what I will present in
this chapter.¹ You can see that I titled it "Sounding the Chord of
Having a Dream." I intend this diagram to be read from the bottom
up, like reading a hexagram from the *I Ching*. The title suggests that we
can also imagine this stack of five cubes sideways, as if they were five keys
on a piano. I think of the stack of cubes as the "Pillar of Isis," relating it
to the Egyptian image of the *djed pillar,* or the Tree of Life.

The image of a pillar brings to mind the backbone of the human body.
But note that I've made the cubes chunky to suggest a full torso, not just
bones, and I want to avoid imposing mind-body schemas such as the
chakras on this "body." Although we indeed can imagine dreams as a kind
of body language, I find that the subtle grammar of dreaming, or even the
distinction between five "keys" on a piano, is far less differentiating of the
"whole" than an imposed body schema might imply.

Having a dream is a whole experience, like hearing a whole chord. As
such, it is difficult to illustrate, let alone talk about, because a dream is
really a *holon,*² meaning that because it is whole in and of itself, it is
autonomous and self-reliant. As a *holon,* simultaneously a dream is part of
a greater whole or wholes—part of the psyche, part of an individual, part
of a person, part of the world. From this perspective, a dream is self-
regulating; it functions first as whole in supraordination to its parts (the
images themselves, the affective experience) and second as a dependent
part in subordination to controls on higher levels (the whole body, the
psyche, one's personal life, Jung's idea of the Self). Let's just say that when

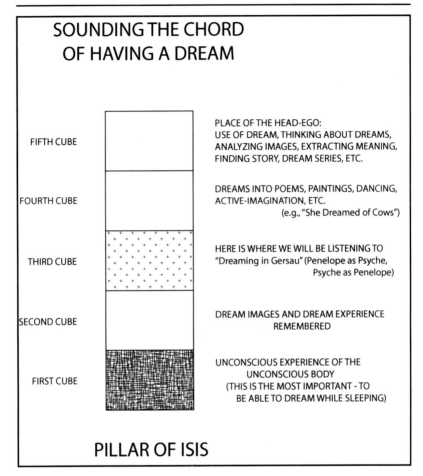

SOUNDING THE CHORD
OF HAVING A DREAM

FIFTH CUBE — PLACE OF THE HEAD-EGO:
USE OF DREAM, THINKING ABOUT DREAMS,
ANALYZING IMAGES, EXTRACTING MEANING,
FINDING STORY, DREAM SERIES, ETC.

FOURTH CUBE — DREAMS INTO POEMS, PAINTINGS, DANCING,
ACTIVE-IMAGINATION, ETC.
(e.g., "She Dreamed of Cows")

THIRD CUBE — HERE IS WHERE WE WILL BE LISTENING TO
"Dreaming in Gersau" (Penelope as Psyche,
Psyche as Penelope)

SECOND CUBE — DREAM IMAGES AND DREAM EXPERIENCE
REMEMBERED

FIRST CUBE — UNCONSCIOUS EXPERIENCE OF THE
UNCONSCIOUS BODY
(THIS IS THE MOST IMPORTANT - TO
BE ABLE TO DREAM WHILE SLEEPING)

PILLAR OF ISIS

Fig. 1

we dream we are having a whole, "just-so" experience that resonates, simultaneously and inexplicably, with other whole, ongoing, "just-so" experiences, as the separate notes of a sounding chord do.

Let's look at the first cube, starting from the bottom up: I've shaded it in to make it dark. It is labeled "The Unconscious Experience of the Unconscious Body: This Is the Most Important."

Once I saw a lovely oriental print depicting a sage leaning against a tiger, both of them with eyes closed, fast asleep. My very first analyst commented that perhaps when we are sound sleep is the only time consciousness and the unconscious peacefully coexist. Yet night after night all of us coexist with our dreams, and if we are fortunate we learn to remember them. Sometimes it feels as if the psyche itself has to learn how to have a coherent dream. I say this to remind you that it takes lived, conscious time to "have a dream-life," which means to be able to experience how the psyche permeates the Pillar of Isis at the second cube, where dream imagery seeps into the light of day. But here at the bottom, in the first cube, the invisible psyche breathes in and out night after night (as well as day after day), dream after dream, whether we ever remember our dreams or not.

The next cube up, the second cube, I have labeled "Dream Images and Dream Experience Remembered." The second cube becomes relevant when we awaken with our body and mind full of a dream or when we inadvertently shake a dream from memory as we make the morning coffee or even as we find a wisp of a dream image returning as we go about our days—interior or "inner" experiences all. Our very sense of time and narration begins in memory, if only within ourselves.

The third cube is marked "Here Is Where We Will Be Listening," and I've made little crosses in it to catch your attention. This cube is the dimension where dream images become clothed in language as we tell them or write them or speak them out loud. Since we've imagined that we are on a Jungian Odyssey, imagine this third dimension as a colorful storeroom of Penelope's threads. Imagine the psyche as Penelope (or Penelope as Psyche) weaving tapestries by day and taking them apart or replacing them by night: our Penelope weaves dream tapestries all night long and undoes them in the morning as she waits for Odysseus—for our heroic egos—to return with our individual lives. This is the realm of the images from which we have collected the raw dream imagery we have shared with each other for the past three mornings, the dreams that I have lightly tended or "pruned" and will read to you in a few moments.

Now notice the fourth cube, stacked on top of the third: in this realm we work the imagery of our dreams and visions into a poem, for example, or we dance our dreams or paint them or have an active imagination with them. Far more ego is involved here, so we don't really have raw dream imagery anymore. Here, from this perspective let us say that while the body has been dreaming, the ego on waking becomes able to harness some of the psyche's (and the body's) creative energy in order to direct it toward personal desires and collective ends.

And the top, the fifth cube: here is where I think we intentionally *use* our dreams, where we *think about* them, and where we analyze the images. Here at the fifth cube is the place where we extract meaning, where we begin to sense an ongoing process in the psyche, where we begin to find story. Here, too, is where a series of dreams begins to make sense, our ability to read them becoming a bit like a dawning ability to read a page of music. This is where we find ourselves in the midst of an ongoing narrative, even though we cannot know the full outlines of the story (the music) and can only know that the bigger picture of many things is beyond our ability to imagine. We can call this fifth cube the place of the head-ego, I suppose— and the place of the analytic or an alchemical relationship.

Now I will share my "Dream Gathering Introduction" and our collection (the dreams gathered), which I simply call "Dreaming in Gersau." Then I will end with a poem. (I don't call "Dreaming in Gersau" a poem at all, for what we have gathered together and I have "tended" and will speak aloud to you is raw dream imagery that is relatively untampered with. The collection simply represents a tapestry of our unconscious imagery over the past three days. Thus we could imagine it as "Penelope's Web.")

By reading Norah Pollard's poem after the dream collection I hope to clarify the important distinction between cube three, where we gather our dreams, and cube four, where creativity begins to color the psyche's discourse.

DREAM-GATHERING INTRODUCTION

To paraphrase a reading of Rumi, think of "the body as night and the soul as day." I think of the heart as a borderland between these two, a liminal space that is animated by spirit both day and night, like we ourselves are and like our dreams. Telling each other our dreams, I suggest, opens this space between and among us.

The images I will recite to you come from our three mornings' gatherings, when those of you who attended were fresh from sleep and willing to share your dreams. When we gather dreams this way, I think that we are actively participating in a worldwide oral tradition of attending to dreams and sharing them that is so old that I imagine it as being rooted in the first waking words of some little *Homo sapiens* child (or whichever of our ancestors first had language), murmured aloud to its mother as they rolled away from each other out of sleep or huddled around an evening fire. As long as we've had words to imagine with and as long as we've had tongue to tell, we've told each other our dreams and listened to each other, catching at whatever stray wisps of image and tendrils of dream we can manage to remember before they fade in morning light.

In "tending" the dreams as lightly as I do, I try to respect the integrity of each dream and each dreamer. Choosing among dreams is like picking up shells along a shore: I lift an image here, an image there, leaving each as intact as possible and seeing how the image falls. It's a kind of pruning process; I don't know what else to call it. When individuals offered more than one dream, I chose among them so that there was space for everyone's dream at least once.

I tried to weave a kind of multicolored garment out of the gathered images, a tapestry that represents the unconscious texture of what I think of as our tribal psyche over the time we've spent together in Gersau. Just as we have been thinking of this time overall as an Odyssey, think of this tapestry as a fabric woven by the psyche, she who stays at home while we wander the day-lit countries of lectures and workshops and the stimulating ideas and stories of our interactions. Beneath all this activity and conversation, psyche remains as "She who weaves within" and awaits our return.

Conferences overflow with words and ideas and conscious experience, and sometimes—to quote a colleague I heard yesterday—"We tend to load the saddlebags on Jesus and let the donkeys roam free."[3] In other words, we become head-heavy—speaking and listening disembodied spirits all. Then, as we think upon raw dream imagery, we are giving body back to what the body can easily bear (our unconscious lives and psyches); this makes our spirits, any spirit, less homesick. Dreams remind us of all the unconscious, equally creative energies that are constantly being generated among all of us as we form and unform our temporary tribes. Thus they ground us in body and spirit as well as psyche, balancing the richness of shared ideas and presence. Jesus and the donkey share the load more evenly. One man once said that for him, hearing the dream images recited back to his group in Ireland (as I will be doing for you in a moment) "captured the perfume" of his personal experience. Another man in India said that his experience of hearing "Dreaming in India" seemed like a form of interpersonal art.

I know that it will be hard to listen attentively, for our thoughts travel about four times faster than clear speech. When we listen to each other speak, our thoughts dart about like fish in the free time left over, focusing on nonverbal cues and signals from the speaker or on what we would like to say next or on what we would like to hear next or wish we had heard instead or on something altogether other-where—all those shadowy undercurrents that we communicate along with our words. Compared to the fullness of ongoing nonverbal experience, language seems very slow.

So please use the time you will find between my words to let your thoughts dart inward rather than out. Forget about analyzing the images you will hear or analyzing me. Fish with your heart, in your heart; fish into, and with, your imagination. Look with your inner eye, listen with your inner ears, and let yourselves re-experience eddies in those deep currents of unconscious feeling that give rise to all our dreams in the first place.

Each dream sails by like a small ship on a river of awareness—a little soul-ship. And as with ships, each dream carries personal cargo. In groups like the one we have shared, we gather the dreams but we do not unpack the personal cargo. Still, personal cargo is there for each dreamer, and if you, as listeners, feel your way into the images you will hear, you will be participating in a shared humanity. For actually, *we* are the little soul-ships, each carrying a cargo of dreams. And each of us sails the psychic reality to which all dreams point—a wild, collective sea of Being, the unseen source of rivers and dreams and ships and people and life and the earth itself, and the universe and the cosmos in which it spins.

But that thought takes us far away. Come back to here and now and rest in an act of listening. Open your senses and recline in the stream of sound. And thank you again for getting up so early in the morning to gather dreams with me.

"Dreaming in Gersau, Switzerland
(23–25 May 2010)"

A blank tablet of fresh clay
and two hands come down on it.
My hands.

In the corner of a basement I build a gift,
an altar of earth.
My friend says her animals,
cats, dogs, walk over it.
The earth has to go, the figures can remain:
a symbolic altar.

Another room, farther down:
Foliage, dark green leaves, cover the walls,
and fern-like branches. How can this be,
With so little light?

Still deeper, another room: in one wall,
a large hole: excavation of an old fire-pit?
Before the hole a wooden, falling-apart,
casket-like box: did it contain a body?
I draw from the box a long wide sheet
of dark grey metal, an imprint at the top

burned black: a little dog, lying on its side.
Heat from this fire must have been intense.

Altering white clothing.
Someone decides
what changes to make.

I walk over a hill and descend deep underground,
through crisscrossing passages, deeper,
to a small basement room, a cooling room
for vegetables. It needs to be bigger,
but the earth would fall in.
As I go deeper, it gets darker. I'm too cold.
I ascend, find a stairway, climb out.

I'm so excited to be home. My brother
brings my parents and my little boy, who looks
like a little old man with stubble—not my son.
Another live figurine also wants to nurse.
I am confused.

In my prayer room-storeroom-kitchen,
I pick up a phone. A voice says
"You must be careful when you travel
because of the work you do.
There is always jealousy."

In high mountains I wander the path
to a lake. Along comes a man in a tractor,
spraying dark, thick, liquid manure.
My white clothes—sprayed!
But I am not bothered. The man lives
in a nearby gypsy camp.

I am writing papers, teaching,
talking about past lives in India.
Someone says
"What do you know about India?
You have never been there."

My driver from Kabul
drives me to New York,
gray and full of dust.
I go from site to site,
ordering piles of carpets.
I wake in shock—Kabul
is in New York!

In the sky, a kite—the tail leads
To a mother and a child,
half in, half out of the womb.

Now I understand the scene in *Death in Venice,*
the orchestra of daemonic figures playing—
that is the demon!
Thomas Mann, you knew everything!

Driving through poverty in South Africa, I am lost.
A couple asks for an uphill lift.
I like the woman, but the man
tells me to leave her behind.
I lie with the man,
and hope my clothing is not stained.
I try to leave
but he has my keys,
and I can't reach my car.

People enter my room: a white-robed figure
sits, yoga-like. He elevates
off the floor.

I'm at a party with friends from a wedding
I attended eight years ago not far from here.

I dreamed of a place before I got there,
so in the dream
I recognized nothing—cows, bells, grass.
Where was I?
Years later, I dream:
high on a hill I see
a cathedral-like building, all the windows lit,
all the doors open,
and snow on the ground beneath it.
I am eager to get there,
but suddenly I am standing in grass with cows,
and cows come to me, and we kiss and nuzzle.
My four-year old granddaughter
takes my hand
and we go down the hill.

Something about a bus
and a change of direction.

Biking in south Switzerland with my children,
we're on a ride in an amusement hall,
going too fast.

Walking along a coastline:
a former relative welcomes me
into his home. It feels good.
Usually he is cold.

To visit a mystic I once knew,
I climb a mountain.
She tries to give me a message.
I remember the Holy Spirit,
and yesterday was Pentecost.

In a strange town, in a strange man's home,
I have to eat dark material. The man has animals
who eat the dark stuff for him.
Do they bite?

Will I inherit a widow's wealth?
Probably not.
Her nephew has a dark gold face
and children, who discuss
and discuss, and discuss.
The Swiss are so rational.
They rarely lose control.
Maybe they do when no one is there.

The earth shuddered last night.
I felt a gentle rocking for a long time.
I ask others, did you feel it?
No one did.[4]

Now I'll end with the poem "She Dreamed of Cows," by Norah Pollard. Remember cube four. You may hear special relevance in this poem because Pollard's poetic imagery resonates with some of the raw imagery from our dreams.

"She Dreamed of Cows"

I knew a woman who washed her hair and bathed her body
and lay down with a .38 in her right hand.
Before she did the thing, she went over her life.
She started at the beginning and recalled everything—
all the shame, sorrow, regret and loss.
This took her a long time into the night

and a long time crying out in rage and grief and disbelief—
until sleep captured her and bore her down.

She dreamed of a green pasture and a green oak tree.
She dreamed of cows. She dreamed she stood
under the tree and the brown and white cows
came slowly up from the pond and stood near her.
Some butted her gently and they licked her bare arms
with their great coarse drooling tongues. Their eyes, wet as
shining water, regarded her.
They came closer and began to
press their warm flanks against her, and as they pressed
an almost unendurable joy came over her and
lifted her like a warm wind and she could fly.
She flew over the tree and she flew over the field and
she flew with the cows.

When the woman woke, she rose and went to the mirror.
She looked a long time at her living self.
Then she went down to the kitchen which the sun had
made all yellow, and she made tea.
She drank it at the table, slowly, all the while
touching her arms where the cows had licked.[5]

NOTES

[1] This essay is a modified version of the talk Robin van Löben Sels gave following the workshop "Dream Gathering" that she presented at the Jungian Odyssey 2010.

[2] Arthur Koestler first used the term *holon* in his nonfiction work *The Ghost in the Machine* (New York: Macmillan, 1968), p. 48.

[3] Dariane Pictet used this phrase in her seminar at the 2010 Jungian Odyssey entitled "Mistrust to Trust in the Works of Rumi, Rilke, and Dickinson." I don't think I'll ever forget it.

[4] The dream images contained here were contributed by the participants in the author's "Dream Gathering" workshop at the Jungian Odyssey 2010. Out of respect for privacy, the contributors remain anonymous. Images gathered by Robin van Löben Sels.

[5] Norah Pollard, "She Dreamed of Cows," in *Death & Rapture in the Animal Kingdom: New Poems by Norah Pollard* (Simsbury, Conn.: Antrim House, 2009), p. 43.

Epilogue

Trust, Betrayal, and Laughter

Doris Lier

Looking into Homer's classic Greek epic poem *The Odyssey*,[1] we find numerous tales of trickery, betrayal, deceit, and intrigue, all of which intrinsically represent the toying with or breaking of trust as we understand it today. The wily maneuvers, which are also displayed in Homer's *The Iliad*,[2] are deployed not only by humans but also by the gods, and of course between gods and humans. But in Greek mythological times, trickery, deception, and other such sly habits are free of weighty guilt and the need for atonement, the kind that came to be associated in Christianity with the one, omnipresent, and punishing God. Indeed the mythological mind often holds connivers to be virtuous. For, as Odysseus says, the "[weaving] of many schemes, / and all sorts of tricks" are required "when [one's] own life's at stake."[3] And when such deeds *are* avenged, punishment is taken in stride as a natural consequence rather than as the upshot of sin or moral transgression.

Accordingly, Odysseus is proudly characterized as a hero of supreme cunning. The Trojan horse, for example, is his idea—a grand deceit that enables the Greeks to conquer Troy. In the fifth song of *The Odyssey*, Odysseus becomes shipwrecked in a heavy storm and is washed ashore on the land of the Phaeacians. As the only survivor of this last catastrophe on the journey home to Ithaca, he is in urgent need of help. The friendly Phaeacians rescue him, treat him to a long rest, and throw a party that welcomes him and bids him farewell at the same time. They offer competitions and prepare a gorgeous banquet with fine food, drinking, singing, laughing, and storytelling.

Odysseus tells the Phaeacians how he outfoxed the one-eyed Cyclops, Polyphemus, and gouged out his eye; how he protected himself against the song of the Sirens by having himself bound to the mast of his ship; and how his hungry shipmates stole and roasted one of Helios's sacred cattle, only to meet with the revenge of death by Zeus's thunderbolt. Not least, Odysseus relays how he tricked the goddess Circe into believing that he was spellproof and then conned her into releasing his shipmates, whom she had transformed into swine. It was for the sake of his comrades, Odysseus maintains, that he gave in to Circe's seduction and shared her bed for a whole year.[4] (And this while his wife Penelope longed for his return to Ithaca.)

But it is not only Odysseus who tells stories. The Phaeacians' blind poet and singer Demodocus entertains Odysseus, too, by recounting thrilling tales, one of which gained worldwide renown. It is a story of a marriage betrayal that evoked Homeric laughter. The beautiful Aphrodite and the lame Hephaestus were married by Zeus's arrangement. Since the marriage had taken place, the gods had feared that Aphrodite's beauty would give cause for jealousy that would disrupt their peace, but they did not view Hephaestus as a threat. Aphrodite disliked being married to the unsightly Hephaestus and so began an affair with Ares, the proud and handsome god of war. They were careless, meeting with each other in Hephaestus's temple. Of course Hephaestus soon discovered their betrayal and began scheming to trap them. Being the most gifted goldsmith the world had ever seen, Hephaestus easily constructed an invisible and unbreakable chain-link net in which the two lovers became ensnared, and their deed was betrayed. Hephaestus summoned all the other gods to view the two lovers. Gathering around the bed, they began "to laugh— / an irrepressible laughter then pealed out /among the blessed gods."[5]

Why might *this* kind of deceit become a laughing matter? Do the gods laugh just for fun or at someone? And if at someone, at whom? At Aphrodite and Ares? At Hephaestos—or at themselves? Such laughter can have many meanings, expressing harmless hilarity, sarcasm, shame, or mockery. But whenever and however it is interpreted, laughter is seldom naive and maybe only rarely holds one single meaning.

The Greek philosopher Aristotle is laughter's advocate. "Mankind . . . is the only one of the animals that laughs," he wrote.[6] With this remark he drew a line between humans and animals and pointed to the power of laughter to express the ambiguous and contradictory nature of human existence, even in the face of betrayal. However, in the early Middle Ages, some began to perceive laughter as the devil's work. They saw laughter as a culpable revelation of one's betrayal of God. This dogma runs against the lived experience that laughter can kill fear and wants to state that "there can be no religion where there is no fear."[7] Led by such belief, John Chrysostom, an archbishop of the early Greek Church, went so far as to preach that Jesus Christ had never laughed.[8]

The medieval motif of forbidden laughter forms the central motive of the murder mystery in *The Name of the Rose*[9] by the Italian author Umberto Eco. Set in the year 1327, the plot unfolds in a fictitious Benedictine monastery in northern Italy. Monks are being murdered, one after the other, and no one understands what is happening in this holy place. Finally it is discovered that the monastery's blind librarian, Jorge von Burgos, had poisoned the pages of a book that he had judged to be highly dangerous and had locked away. The book was the very last copy of the second part of Aristotle's *Poetics*—a treatise on comedy![10] The monks who discovered the book died when they licked their fingers to turn the pages. Here we have a librarian and man of the cloth who became as wily and deceitful a character as any in Homer in the name of guarding the faith.

During this Jungian Odyssey you explored seriously many kinds of betrayal and deceit and probably identified with their agonies. Perhaps, too, you experienced the laughter that wells up with a dawning of consciousness in a moment of self-recognition or discovery of new truth. This evening's farewell party is our last chance to tell stories and laugh with each other about such shadowy sides of human life. Laughter is finally, as we say in German, "the salt in the soup"—the ingredient that rounds off our human woes.

In this spirit I wish you a joyful round-off—with pleasurable eating, drinking, laughing, dancing, and storytelling. And I wish you a good and safe journey home. By the way: After their own farewell party, the Phaeacians set sail toward Ithaca, transporting Odysseus, who slept the whole way. They delivered him home by night, stealing in through a hidden harbor. Homer does not explain the circumstances, but we can assume that our hero was happily drunk.

NOTES

[Editors' note: This epilogue is an abbreviated version of the author's farewell address, given at the closing banquet of Jungian Odyssey 2010. The references that follow supplement the talk.]

¹ Homer, *The Odyssey,* trans. Ian Johnston, 2nd ed. (Arlington, Va.: Richer Resources Publications, 2007).

² Homer, *The Iliad,* trans. Ian Johnston, 2nd ed. (Arlington, Va.: Richer Resources Publications, 2007).

³ "Book 9: Ismarus, The Lotus Eaters, and the Cyclops," in Homer, *The Odyssey,* p. 179, lines 556–558.

⁴ "Book 10: Aeolus, the Laestrygonians, and Circe," in *ibid.,* pp. 192–204, lines 195–603.

⁵ "Book 8: Odysseus Is Entertained in Phaeacia," in *ibid.,* p. 153, lines 410–412.

⁶ Aristotle, "Book III," in *On the Parts of Animals,* trans. James G. Lennox (Oxford: Oxford University Press, 2001), p. 69, lines 6–7.

⁷ Lactantius, "A Treatise on the Anger of God. Addressed to Donatus," in *The Ante-Nicene Fathers,* vol. 7, *Fathers of the Third and Fourth Century,* ed. Alexander Roberts, James Donaldson, and Arthur Cleveland Cox (1886; repr., New York: Cosimo Inc., 2007), p. 269.

⁸ Jutta Tloka, *Griechische Christen, christliche Griechen, Studien und Texte zu Antike und Christentum* (Tübingen: Mohr Siebeck, 2005), pp. 148–149. [Editors' note: See also Ingvild Sælid Gilhus, *Laughing Gods, Weeping Virgins: Laughter in the History of Religion* (London: Routledge, 2009), p. 62.]

⁹ Umberto Eco, *The Name of the Rose,* trans. William Weaver (New York: Harcourt Brace Jovanovich, 1983).

¹⁰ The "rediscovery" of Aristotle's treatise on comedy is Eco's invention. In *On Rhetoric,* Aristotle does in fact refer the reader to a complete treatise on comedy contained in his *Poetics.* However the treatise is lost, as no extant copy of *Poetics* includes it. See Aristotle, *On Rhetoric: A Theory of Civic Discourse,* trans. George A. Kennedy (New York: Oxford University Press, 1991), Book 1, Chapter 11, §39; and Book 3, Chapter 18, §7.

Editors

Stacy Wirth, M.A., graduated from the C. G. Jung Institute Zurich
(2003) after earning her MA in the psychology of art from Antioch
University (1997). Her bachelor's studies in dance and anthropology
were completed at Mills College in California (1977). In 1991 she
shared the Zurich Mayor's Counsel Culture Prize for dance. Since
2004 she has served on the AGAP Executive Committee, and she
became co-president in 2010. She is a training analyst at
ISAPZURICH and co-chair of the Jungian Odyssey Committee. She
conducts her private analytical practice in Zurich.

Isabelle Meier, Dr. Phil., is a graduate of the C. G. Jung Institute Zurich
and maintains a private practice in Zurich. She further trained as a
Guided Affective Imagery (GAI) therapist. As a faculty member of
ISAPZURICH, she serves as a training analyst, supervisor, and co-
chair of the Jungian Odyssey Committee. She co-edited *Seele und
Forschung* [*Soul and Research*] (Bern: Karger Verlag, 2006) and is the
Swiss editor for the German edition of the *Journal of Analytical
Psychology.* Her special area of interest is the links between
imagination, complexes, and archetypes.

John Hill, M.A., received his degrees in philosophy at the University of
Dublin and the Catholic University of America. He trained at the C.
G. Jung Institute Zurich, has practiced as a Jungian analyst since 1973,
and is a training analyst and supervisor at ISAPZURICH. He has
published articles on the association experiment, Celtic myth, James
Joyce, dreams, the significance of home, and Christian mysticism.
He is the author of *At Home in the World: Sounds and Symmetries of
Belonging* (Spring Journal Books, 2010).

Contributors

Diane Cousineau Brutsche, Ph.D, was born in Montreal, Canada. She earned a doctorate in French literature from the University of Paris and a diploma in analytical psychology from the C. G. Jung Institute Zurich. She works as an analyst in private practice in Zurich and is a training analyst, supervisor, and lecturer at ISAPZURICH.

John Desteian, J.D., D. Psy, graduated from the C. G. Jung Institute Zurich in 1983. He is co-president of the Association of Graduate Analytical Psychologists (AGAP) and a licensed psychologist in private practice in St. Paul, Minnesota. His publications include a book and articles on relationships, creativity, politics, and semantics. Presently, he is working on two books: one concerning phenomenology, hermeneutics, and ontology and the other examining the role of collective consciousness in the political life of the United States.

Deborah Egger-Biniores, M.S.W, is a training analyst at ISAPZURICH. She maintains a private practice in Stäfa. She was president of AGAP from 2001 to 2010. Her professional areas of interest include adult development, transferential fields, and spiritual growth. She is currently writing on the role of the couple in adult development.

Allan Guggenbühl, Prof. Dr. Phil., received his degrees from the University of Zurich in education and psychology and a diploma from the C. G. Jung Institute Zurich. He is director of the Institute for Conflict Management in Bern and is well known for his method of Mythodrama and Crisis Intervention in Swiss schools. He has many publications, including his celebrated *Men, Power, and Myths: The Quest for Male Identity* (Continuum, 1997).

Donald Kalsched, Ph.D., is a Jungian analyst and licensed clinical psychologist who has a private practice in Albuquerque, New Mexico. He is a senior faculty member and supervisor with the Inter-Regional Society of Jungian Analysts. His major book, *The Inner World of Trauma: Archetypal Defenses of the Personal Spirit* (Routledge, 1996), explores the interface between contemporary psychoanalytic theory and Jungian theory as it relates to clinical work with the survivors of early childhood trauma. Currently, he is at work on a new book, *Trauma and the Soul.*

Doris Lier, Lic. Phil., holds a diploma in analytical psychology from the C. G. Jung Institute Zurich. Since 1988 she has had a private practice in Zurich and is currently a training analyst, supervisor, and lecturer at ISAPZURICH. She has published articles about analytical psychology, the history of symbols, and epistemology.

Christian Roesler, Prof. Dr. Dipl. Psych., is Professor of Clinical Psychology at the Catholic University of Applied Sciences in Freiburg, Germany; a Jungian psychoanalyst in private practice in Freiburg; and a member of the faculties of the C. G. Jung Institutes in Stuttgart and Zurich. He specializes in work with couples and families and in interpretive research methods. His research and publications cover such areas as analytical psychology and contemporary sciences, couples counseling, postmodern identity construction, narrative research, and media psychology.

Judith Savage, LICSW, LMFT, is a Jungian analyst in private practice in St. Paul, Minnesota, a licensed independent clinical social worker, and a marriage and family therapist. She has been on the Board of Directors of the Minnesota Association of Marriage and Family Therapists, she is a past executive officer of the Inter-Regional Society of Jungian Analysts, and she is currently a member of the society's Training Committee. She is the author of *Mourning Unlived Lives: A Psychological Study of Childbearing Loss* (Chiron, 1989) and a contributor to *The Soul of Popular Culture: Looking at Contemporary Heroes, Myths, and Monsters* (Open Court, 1998). A former coordinator and treasurer of the Minnesota Seminar in Jungian Studies, she is currently a member of its core faculty.

Murray Stein, Ph.D., is the president of and a training analyst at ISAPZURICH. From 2001 to 2004 he served as president of the International Association for Analytical Psychology (IAAP). He is a founding member of two IAAP societies: the Inter-Regional Society for Jungian Analysts (United States) and the Chicago Society of Jungian Analysts. He is the author of *Jung's Treatment of Christianity* (Chiron, 1985); *In Midlife: A Jungian Perspective* (Spring, 2009); *Transformation: Emergence of the Self* (TAMU Press, 2004); and *Jung's Map of the Soul* (Open Court, 1998). He is the editor of *Jungian Analysis* (Open Court, 1994) and co-editor of the Chiron Clinical Series.

Robin van Löben Sels, Ph.D., was born in California. She received her doctorate in psychiatry and religion from Union Theological Seminary in New York City, is a graduate of the C. G. Jung Institute of New York, and attended the Jung Institute in Zurich when it was still on Gemeindestrasse. She recently moved from the East Coast with her husband, Donald Kalsched, to live in Albuquerque, New Mexico, where she continues a limited practice, supervision, and teaching. Her professional affiliations include the Inter-Regional Association of Jungian Analysts and IAAP. She is the author of *A Dream in the World* (Routledge, 2003) as well as several articles and a book of poetry.

Joanne Wieland-Burston, Ph.D., has conducted her private analytical practice in Germany since 1988, after having worked for nine years as an analyst in Switzerland. She is currently on the faculty of ISAPZURICH. After graduating from the C. G. Jung Institute Zurich in 1981, she worked there as a training analyst from 1991 to 2005. In 1999 she organized a supervision group that brings together therapists from various schools to discuss the impact of the Nazi period on clients in Germany. This is among her special interests and the topic of lectures she has held in many countries and schools.

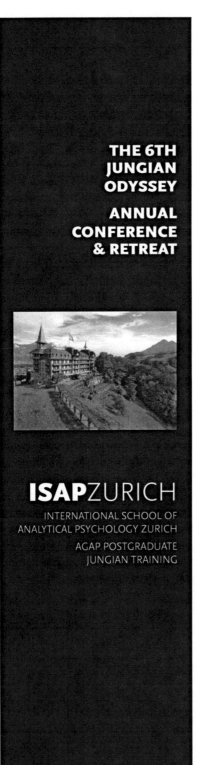

THE 6TH
JUNGIAN
ODYSSEY

ANNUAL
CONFERENCE
& RETREAT

ISAPZURICH
INTERNATIONAL SCHOOL OF
ANALYTICAL PSYCHOLOGY ZURICH
AGAP POSTGRADUATE
JUNGIAN TRAINING

VALLEYS OF DESPAIR, MOUNTAINS OF BLISS

Measuring the Forces of Destiny

June 9-16, 2012
Hotel Pax Montana
Flüeli Ranft,
Switzerland

With
Ann Ulanov, PhD
James Hollis, PhD
and Faculty
of ISAPZURICH

www.isapzurich.com
info@jungianodyssey.ch

SPRING JOURNAL BOOKS

THE BOOK PUBLISHING IMPRINT OF *SPRING JOURNAL*,
THE OLDEST JUNGIAN PSYCHOLOGY JOURNAL IN THE WORLD

HOW TO ORDER:

MAIL: SPRING JOURNAL BOOKS, 627 URSULINES STREET # 7,
NEW ORLEANS, LOUISIANA 70116, USA
TELEPHONE: (504) 524-5117
WEBSITE: WWW.SPRINGJOURNALANDBOOKS.COM

STUDIES IN ARCHETYPAL PSYCHOLOGY SERIES
SERIES EDITOR: GREG MOGENSON

Collected English Papers, *Wolfgang Giegerich*
   Vol. 1: *The Neurosis of Psychology: Primary Papers Towards a Critical Psychology*, ISBN 978-1-882670-42-0, 284 pp., $20.00
   Vol. 2: *Technology and the Soul: From the Nuclear Bomb to the World Wide Web*, ISBN 978-1-882670-43-4, 356 pp., $25.00
   Vol. 3: *Soul-Violence*, ISBN 978-1-882670-44-4, 476 pp., $32.95
   Vol. 4: *The Soul Always Thinks,* ISBN 978-1-882670-45-1, 620 pp. $32.95

Dialectics & Analytical Psychology: The El Capitan Canyon Seminar, Wolfgang Giegerich, David L. Miller, and Greg Mogenson, ISBN 978-1-882670-92-5, 136 pp., $20.00

Northern Gnosis: Thor, Baldr, and the Volsungs in the Thought of Freud and Jung, Greg Mogenson, ISBN 978-1-882670-90-1, 140 pp., $20.00

Raids on the Unthinkable: Freudian and Jungian Psychoanalyses, Paul Kugler, ISBN 978-1-882670-91-8, 160 pp., $20.00

The Essentials of Style: A Handbook for Seeing and Being Seen, Benjamin Sells, ISBN 978-1-882670-68-0, 165 pp., $21.95

The Wounded Researcher: A Depth Psychological Approach to Research, Robert Romanyshyn, ISBN 978-1-882670-47-5, 360 pp., $24.95

The Sunken Quest, the Wasted Fisher, the Pregnant Fish: Postmodern Reflections on Depth Psychology, Ronald Schenk, ISBN 978-1-882670-48-2, 166 pp., $20.00

Fire in the Stone: The Alchemy of Desire, Stanton Marlan, ed., ISBN 978-1-882670-49-3, 176 pp., $22.95

After Prophecy: Imagination, Incarnation, and the Unity of the Prophetic Tradition, Tom Cheetham, ISBN 978-1-882670-81-9, 183 pp., $22.95

Archetypal Psychologies: Reflections in Honor of James Hillman, Stanton Marlan, ed., ISBN 978-1-882670-54-3, 526 pp. $32.95

JUNGIAN ODYSSEY SERIES
SERIES EDITORS: STACY WIRTH, ISABELLE MEIER, AND JOHN HILL

Volume I
Intimacy: Venturing the Uncertainties of the Heart, Isabelle Meier, Stacy Wirth, and John Hill, eds., ISBN 978-1-882670-84-0, 225 pp., $24.95

Volume II
Destruction and Creation: Facing the Ambiguities of Power, Isabelle Meier, Stacy Wirth, and John Hill, eds., ISBN: 978-1-935528-06-7, 225 pp., $24.95

ZURICH LECTURE SERIES IN ANALYTICAL PSYCHOLOGY SERIES
SERIES EDITORS: NANCY CATER AND MURRAY STEIN

At Home in the World: Sounds and Symmetries of Belonging, John Hill ISBN: 978-1-935528-00-5, 288 pp., $26.95.

ANALYTICAL PSYCHOLOGY & CONTEMPORARY CULTURE SERIES
SERIES EDITOR: THOMAS SINGER, M.D.

Psyche and the City: A Soul's Guide to the Modern Metropolis, Thomas Singer, ed., ISBN: 978-1-935528-03-6, 420 pp., $32.95

Violence in History, Culture, and the Psyche, Luigi Zoja, ISBN 978-1-882670-50-5, 160 pp., $23.95

MORE SPRING JOURNAL BOOKS

Disturbances in the Field: Essays in Honor of David L. Miller, Christine Downing, ed., ISBN 978-1-882670-37-6, 318 pp., $23.95

Three Faces of God: Traces of the Trinity in Literature and Life, David L. Miller, ISBN 978-1-882670-94-9, 197 pp., $20.00

Christs: Meditations on Archetypal Images in Christian Theology, David L. Miller, ISBN 978-1-882670-93-2, 249 pp., $20.00

Hells and Holy Ghosts: A Theopoetics of Christian Belief, David L. Miller, ISBN 978-1-882670-97-0, 238 pp., $20.00

Electra: Tracing a Feminine Myth through the Western Imagination, Nancy Cater, ISBN 978-1-882670-98-7, 137 pp., $20.00

Fathers' Daughters: Breaking the Ties That Bind, Maureen Murdock, ISBN 978-1-882670-31-4, 258 pp., $20.00

Daughters of Saturn: From Father's Daughter to Creative Woman, Patricia Reis, ISBN 978-1-882670-32-1, 361 pp., $23.95

Women's Mysteries: Toward a Poetics of Gender, Christine Downing, ISBN 978-1-882670-99-4, 237 pp., $20.00

Gods in Our Midst: Mythological Images of the Masculine—A Woman's View, Christine Downing, ISBN 978-1-882670-28-4, 152 pp., $20.00

Journey through Menopause: A Personal Rite of Passage, Christine Downing, ISBN 978-1-882670-33-8, 172 pp., $20.00

Psyche's Sisters: Reimagining the Meaning of Sisterhood, Christine Downing, ISBN 978-1-882670-74-1, 177 pp., $20.00

Portrait of the Blue Lady: The Character of Melancholy, Lyn Cowan, ISBN 978-1-882670-96-3, 314 pp., $23.95

Field, Form, and Fate: Patterns in Mind, Nature, and Psyche, Michael Conforti, ISBN 978-1-882670-40-6, 181 pp., $20.00

The Betrayal of the Soul in Psychotherapy, Robert Stein, ISBN 978-1-882670-16-1, 195 pp., $19.00

Love, Sex, and Marriage: Collected Essays of Robert Stein, Robert Stein, ISBN 978-1-882670-20-8, 382 pp. $19.00

Dark Voices: The Genesis of Roy Hart Theatre, Noah Pikes, ISBN 978-1-882670-19-2, 155 pp., $20.00

The World Turned Inside Out: Henry Corbin and Islamic Mysticism, Tom Cheetham, ISBN 978-1-882670-24-6, 210 pp., $20.00

Teachers of Myth: Interviews on Educational and Psychological Uses of Myth with Adolescents, Maren Tonder Hansen, ISBN 978-1-882670-89-5, 73 pp., $15.95

Following the Reindeer Woman: Path of Peace and Harmony, Linda Schierse Leonard, ISBN 978-1-882670-95-6, 229 pp., $20.00

An Oedipus—The Untold Story: A Ghostly Mythodrama in One Act, Armando Nascimento Rosa, ISBN 978-1-882670-38-3, 103 pp., $20.00

The Dreaming Way: Dreamwork and Art for Remembering and Recovery, Patricia Reis and Susan Snow, ISBN 978-1-882670-46-8, 174 pp. $24.95

Living with Jung: "Enterviews" with Jungian Analysts, Volume 1, Robert and Janis Henderson, ISBN 978-1-882670-35-2, 225 pp., $21.95

Living with Jung: "Enterviews" with Jungian Analysts, Volume 2, Robert and Janis Henderson, ISBN 978-1-882670-72-7, 275 pp., $23.95

Living with Jung: "Enterviews" with Jungian Analysts, Volume 3, Robert and Janis Henderson, ISBN 978-1-935528-05-0, 324 pp., $23.95

Terraspychology: Re-engaging the Soul of Place, Craig Chalquist, ISBN 978-1-882670-65-9, 158 pp., $21.95

Psyche and the Sacred: Spirituality beyond Religion, Lionel Corbet, ISBN 978-1-882670-34-5, 350 pp., $23.95

Brothers and Sisters: Discovering the Psychology of Companionship, Lara Newton, ISBN 978-1-882670-70-1, 310 pp., $24.95

Evocations of Absence: Multidisciplinary Perspectives on Void States, Paul W. Ashton, ed., ISBN 978-1-882670-75-8, 214 pp., $22.95

Clio's Circle: Entering The Imaginal World of Historians, Ruth Meyer, ISBN 978-1-882670-70-3, 325 pp., $23.95

Sexuality and the Religious Imagination, Bradley A. TePaske, ISBN: 978-1-882670-51-2, 299 pp., $27.95

Mortally Wounded: Stories of Soul Pain, Death, and Healing, Michael Kearney, ISBN 978-1-882670-79-6, 157 pp., $19.95

Dream Tending, Stephen Aizenstat, ISBN 978-0-882670-55-0, 287 pp., $38.00 (hardcover)

The War of the Gods in Addiction: C. G. Jung, Alcoholics Anonymous, and Archetypal Evil, David E. Schoen, ISBN 978-1-882670-57-4, 172 pp., $23.95

C. G. Jung and the Sioux Traditions: Dreams, Visions, Nature, and the Primitive, Vine Deloria, Jr., edited by Philip J. Deloria and Jerome S. Bernstein, ISBN 978-1-882670-61-1, 292 pp., $25.95

Reimagining Education: Essays on Reviving the Soul of Learning, Dennis Patrick Slattery and Jennifer Leigh Selig, eds., ISBN 978-1-882670-63-5, 212 pp., $25.95

Imagination & Medicine: The Future of Healing in an Age of Neuroscience, Stephen Aizenstat and Robert Bosnak, eds., ISBN 978-1-882670-62-8, 212 pp., $24.95

A Place of Healing: Working with Nature & Soul at the End of Life, Michael Kearney, M.D., ISBN 978-1-882670-58-1, 292 pp., $23.95

Woman Changing Woman: Restoring the Mother-Daughter Relationship, Virginia Beane Rutter, ISBN 978-1-882670-83-3, 303 pp., $25.95

The Call to Create: Listening to the Muse in Art and Everyday Life, Linda Schierse Leonard, ISBN 978-1-935528-01-2, 285 pp., $26.95

By Grief Transformed: Dreams and the Mourning Process, Susan Olson, ISBN 978-1-882670-77-2, 276 pp., $24.95

Kabbalistic Visions: C.G. Jung and Jewish Mysticism, Sanford L. Drob, ISBN 978-1-882670-86-4, 332 pp., $26.95

C. G. Jung in the Humanities: Taking the Soul's Path, Susan Rowland, ISBN 978-1-935528-02-9, 190 pp., $24.95

Music and Psyche: Contemporary Psychoanalytic Explorations, Paul Ashton and Stephen Bloch, eds., ISBN: 978-1-935528-04-3, 325 pp. $26.95.

Mary of Magdala: A Gnostic Fable, Armando Nascimento Rosa with an Introduction by Veronica Goodchild and Essays about Mary Magdalene by Susan Rowland, Nancy Qualls-Corbett, Bradley A. TePaske, Sally Porterfield, António Mercado, and Rosamonde Miller, ISBN: 978-1-882670-52-9, 136 pp., $20.00

The Memoir of Tina Keller-Jenny: A Lifelong Confrontation with the Psychology of C.G. Jung, Wendy Swan, ed., with a Foreword by Sonu Shamdasani, ISBN: 978-1-882670-85-7, 170 pp., $23.95

A True Note on a Slack String: The Poetry of Patrick Kavanagh and the Psychology of C.G. Jung—An Imaginal Basis for Therapeutic Change, Reamonn O'Donnchadha, ISBN: 978-1-882670-47-5, 250 pp., $24.95

CPSIA information can be obtained at www.ICGtesting.com

264886BV00004B/6/P